PLATO'S *REPUBLIC:*

Interpretation and Criticism

WADSWORTH STUDIES IN
PHILOSOPHICAL CRITICISM
Alexander Sesonske, General Editor

HUMAN UNDERSTANDING:
Studies in the Philosophy of David Hume

META-*MEDITATIONS:*
Studies in Descartes

PLATO'S *MENO:*
Text and Criticism

PLATO'S *REPUBLIC:*
Interpretation and Criticism

LIMITS OF LIBERTY:
Studies of Mill's *On Liberty*

PLATO'S *REPUBLIC:*

Interpretation and Criticism

edited by
Alexander Sesonske
UNIVERSITY OF CALIFORNIA, SANTA BARBARA

Wadsworth Publishing Company, Inc.
BELMONT, CALIFORNIA

WADSWORTH STUDIES IN PHILOSOPHICAL CRITICISM

The idea of a series of Studies in Philosophical Criticism developed in response to a growing problem in American universities. Philosophy can be taught most successfully in small classes; philosophical understanding grows in the course of a dialogue where problems are discussed from diverse points of view by men who differ in experience and temperament. But with the increase in college enrollments, the size of introductory classes has grown larger and the possibility of a dialogue between professor and students more remote. The hope is that the Studies in Philosophical Criticism will make a dialogue of sorts possible in a class of a hundred, or a thousand, as well as in smaller classes and seminars. Each volume in the series contains a collection of critical writings related to a single classical philosophical text, such as Descartes' *Meditations* or Plato's *Republic*. These critical writings are not substitutes for the classical work, but supplements to it. They should be read in conjunction with the classical text. So used, they will bring to bear on the problems raised by Descartes, Hume, or Plato that diversity of voices and viewpoints which is the heart of the dialogue—and also, it is hoped, will prompt the student to add his voice to the discussion.

In selecting material for the volumes in the series, the editor has not searched primarily for writings that provide a definitive analysis of the classical text, but has rather selected those papers he thought might be most useful in undergraduate courses in philosophy, both to provoke students into serious engagement with the text and the problems found there, and to present them with a variety of philosophical styles and idioms. Most of the writings reprinted are quite contemporary; they were selected not only for their excellence but also as an indication that many of the classical problems of philosophy persist as centers of current controversy. It is believed that this format also achieves one prime desideratum: it acquaints the student both with the great works of the philosophical tradition and with the most contemporary concepts, techniques, and modes of thought.

CONTENTS

PLATO'S *REPUBLIC:*
Interpretation and Criticism

INTRODUCTION

Alfred North Whitehead once wrote that all of Western philosophy is but a series of footnotes to Plato—an exaggeration, perhaps, but not wildly wrong. Plato lived in the 4th century B.C., very near the beginning of Western philosophic thought. We know that he was influenced by his predecessors, Heraclitus, Parmenides, the Sophists and Pythagoreans, and particularly by Socrates, his acknowledged master; two hundred years of remarkable intellectual activity in Greece contribute to the depth and complexity of Plato's thought. Still, no earlier *writer* left anything like Plato's wide-ranging, deep-probing, closely reasoned body of work, and we may well doubt that any *thinker* before Plato had undertaken such a comprehensive consideration of man and the universe. Starting from Socrates' attempt to define the "virtues," those moral traits whose achievement constituted excellence in human character, Plato learned that the kind of knowledge Socrates sought would not result from a mere continuation of the Socratic examination of what ordinary people say about courage or temperance or justice. Rather, the inquiry must be broadened to include questions of logic, the possibility and nature of knowledge, God and politics and poetry—ultimately to include almost every aspect of man, the institutions that define his life, and the universe within which this life occurs.

Thus Plato was led to explore the whole of human knowledge and to raise most of the major questions with which Western philosophers have since been concerned. His answers are often tentative; put forth in one dialogue, only to be discarded or ignored in another. Modern thinkers generally reject what they call "Plato's philosophy": taking Plato to have arrived at a systematic solution of his problems, they find this solution unacceptable. But the status of Plato as the greatest of Western philosophers lies not in the soundness of the answers he provides, but rather in his unequaled perception of what questions must be asked, in his shaping of the language to allow the asking, and in the vast range of possibilities suggested in his exploration of every major problem.

Of all Plato's writings, the *Republic* is no doubt the best-known and most influential single work. The most comprehensive of Plato's dialogues, it has been said to contain the first important theoretical

1

statement in such diverse areas as education, political science, psychology, aesthetics, and theology. Some have hailed it as the foundation stone of higher education and the first Utopia; others have denounced it as the blueprint for a totalitarian state. It begins with a commonplace scene and a Socratic question, "What is justice?" and ends with a vision of the soul's career after death. In style it varies from highly abstract argument to metaphor and allegory, from straightforward exposition to poetic myth. Its variety, its comprehensiveness, and the controversial nature of its contents combine to make the *Republic* an admirable introduction to philosophy. The student who reads it with care, who tries to understand why each major turn in the argument occurs when and as it does, and who attempts to discover what can be said about each view put forth, will have encountered many of the central problems of philosophy and will perhaps see why these problems persist today as matters of concern.

In the present volume I have sought primarily to include writings comprehensible and useful to students in an introductory philosophy class. It is impossible, of course, to include in a volume of this size a discussion of all the significant topics in the *Republic;* I have thought it better to provide deeper coverage of the major themes than to offer a scattering of articles about interesting but peripheral matters.

The first four selections are concerned primarily with Book I of the *Republic.* This may seem excessive, since the *Republic* contains ten books, but Book I is probably the most difficult portion of the *Republic* for beginning students; it presents the major problem and several of the major themes of the whole work, and it is the only section of the *Republic* that exemplifies at length what has become known as the "Socratic method." The four papers in this group exhibit four quite different approaches to the *Republic,* four "styles" of inquiry, no one of which by itself is sufficient to display the depth and richness of Plato's work.

The first paper, H. W. B. Joseph's "The Argument with Polemarchus," contains a detailed examination of a short section of Book I, the first serious argument in the *Republic* about the concept "justice." Joseph carefully sorts the strands of this argument for us, contending that it is not captious and unfair but that it soundly refutes the view that justice consists in the performance of a series of specifiable acts. In his treatment of this passage, Joseph provides an example of how a Platonic dialogue should be read: noting the assumptions implicit in the opening moves, taking account of each turn in the argument, questioning Socrates' intentions when he introduces a new consideration, noting how Polemarchus should have responded had he been fully aware of the direction of Socrates' thought. All this reminds us that it is characteristic of Socrates' method not to tell his hearers what to believe but to lead them by a series of questions to think through the problem for themselves. Plato, in writing Socratic dialogues, similarly intended to provoke questions rather than to provide answers, to initiate the philosophic quest rather than to conclude it.

Ernest Barker, in considering "Thrasymachus' Conception of Justice," proceeds quite differently. Instead of examining the argument in detail, Barker seeks to formulate a clear and careful statement of the view espoused by the Sophist, to note its attractiveness and its falsity, and to indicate the line of Socrates' "refutation" of this view in Book I. The argument Barker notes as "of supreme importance" in this section provides the subject matter for our third paper, H. S. Thayer's "Plato: The Theory and Language of Function." Thayer discusses this short argument in detail, but goes beyond this to deal with *function*, the key concept in the argument. Thayer's discussion clarifies the concept of *function*, shows its relation to other central Platonic concepts, and finally relates this strand of Plato's thought to a problem much argued in twentieth-century philosophy—that of the function of language.

The final paper in this group deals with a quite different aspect of Book I; its concern is not the philosophic argument but the dramatic framework within which this argument occurs. In "Plato's Apology: *Republic* I" Alexander Sesonske contends that this dramatic framework provides the clue for understanding the relation between Book I and the remainder of the *Republic*. Socrates in Book I is the ironic probing gadfly of the early dialogues, a man who always questions and never claims to know, the master of the "Socratic method" whose mission was to bring his fellow Athenians to recognize and acknowledge their own ignorance, an ignorance he himself openly professes. In Book II of the *Republic* a new Socrates appears, confident and knowing, prepared to solve any problem his friends may propose. When this Socrates asks questions, they are merely perfunctory, serving only to elicit agreement with the doctrine he is expounding. In his short paper Sesonske attempts to show the reasons for this change.

At the close of Book I Thrasymachus has been silenced, but the question "What is justice?" remains unanswered. The argument is revived by Glaucon and Adeimantus, who restate Thrasymachus' view in a more plausible form and demand that Socrates demonstrate its falsity. Richard Lewis Nettleship, in "Statement of the Problem of the *Republic*," presents a masterful exposition of this segment of Plato's work. Nettleship states clearly the views expressed, analyzes some of the critical concepts (such as *nature* and *convention*), and discusses the "real and important facts" that seem to support these false theories. He attempts, in short, to exhibit the full force of the challenge made to Socrates, and both the necessity and difficulty of responding to it.

The following two papers discuss Plato's answer to this challenge: the conception of justice developed in Socrates' construction of the ideal state. H. A. Prichard distinguishes several aspects of Plato's treatment of justice, shows what Plato's view must be if it is to be consistent, and then questions whether, on this view, it could be shown that the just man must be happier than the unjust. In a final section he discusses the theory of motivation that, he holds, made it necessary for Plato to contend that we must gain by performing just acts. David Sachs, in "A Fallacy in Plato's *Republic*," argues that there are two conceptions of justice in the *Republic*, a "vulgar" conception and a "Platonic" one. He claims that these are quite different and that Plato's failure to bridge this difference dooms his attempt to answer the challenge issued by Glaucon and Adeimantus in Book II.

We turn then from the moral to the political level of the *Republic*. Socrates proposes such radical reforms as the equality of women and the abolition both of private property and of the family among the ruling classes of the ideal state. These reforms and the conceptions that led Plato to propose them are discussed by Ernest Barker in "Communism in Plato's *Republic*." An organic view of the state and a closely related conception of the human self are crucial elements of Plato's political theory. Barker assesses both the truth and the falsity of these conceptions and provides a balanced criticism of the reactionary tendencies often noted in Plato's political thought.

At the heart of the *Republic* (in Books VI and VII) are several obscure but important passages, which constitute the major expression (in the *Republic*) of Plato's metaphysics and theory of knowledge. The first of these passages discusses the Idea (or Form) of the Good as the ultimate object of knowledge, comparing this Idea to the sun and its role in the world of vision. This comparison is discussed by Sir David Ross, who finds the comparison most intelligible as an expression of the relation of the Idea of Good to other *ethical* ideas and rejects the notion that the comparison justifies identification of the Idea of Good with God. The second passage is Plato's analysis of the Divided Line, which sums up the many passages in earlier dialogues contrasting ignorance and knowledge, appearance and reality. In "The Four Stages of Intelligence" Richard Lewis Nettleship analyzes this symbol of the four levels of human awareness distinguished by Plato and makes clear both the state of mind and its object at each level.

Running through the *Republic* are references to poetry and poets. Everyone from Cephalus to Socrates cites passages of poetry as support for his ideas; the discussion of the ideal state becomes an analysis of poetic style, and when the argument seems to be concluded, Socrates returns to the subject of poetry, formulates what may be the first aesthetic theory, and then proclaims the banishment of poets from the ideal state. All this concern with poetry in a work whose major question seems to be "What is justice?" should surprise us. So, at least, claims Eric Havelock in "Plato on Poetry." Even more, we should be puzzled by the violence of Plato's attack on poetry, which seems, in Plato's view, to have some awesome power. In summing up Plato's treatment of poetry and showing why he accords it such importance, Havelock aids our understanding of the *Republic* in several ways. He shows its relation to contemporary Greek culture; he draws together the many strands of the work more completely than any other writer in this volume; he discusses at some length a major aspect of the *Republic* barely touched on in our other essays: its treatment of education. And in the second half of his paper, Havelock traces the development of one of the central concepts in Plato's philosophy, *mimesis*—a concept which was to remain the dominant notion in Western aesthetics for two thousand years.

Surprisingly, Plato turns at the end of the *Republic* from a denunciation of poetry to the creation of a poetic myth, the myth of Er, which forsakes all argument and depicts the condition of the soul after death. In our final paper I. M. Crombie discusses why Plato appended such flights of poetic fancy to the wiry argument of many dialogues to provide, perhaps, a kind of insight argument cannot achieve. If nothing else, this final myth and Crombie's discussion of it should add to our awareness of the complexity of Plato's thought and make us hesitate to accept any interpretation of it as final and complete.

A. S.

PLATO'S *REPUBLIC*:
THE ARGUMENT
WITH POLEMARCHUS*

H.W.B. Joseph

I remember being much puzzled and dissatisfied with the first book of Plato's *Republic,* when I first read it; and I do not suppose the experience to be uncommon. The writing is brilliant, the dramatic interest greater than anywhere later in the work. But the argument is elusive, and in places has an appearance of being scarcely serious, or even unfair. Yet the book is one on which, if we may judge by the story of his having rewritten the opening of it ten times, Plato spent great care, and we can hardly suppose that he cared only about the style; he must have thought that the arguments which Socrates is made to bring against what he (Socrates) thinks are false doctrines about Justice and Injustice, before developing his own, were sound arguments; why else, in a dialogue of such importance, should they have been allowed to stand? The book may be earlier in date than those which follow. This view about it has strong support from 'stylometric' investigations, besides being suggested by obvious differences between it and the rest, and obvious resemblances of it to dialogues of the so-called 'Socratic' group, like the *Charmides* or *Laches.* One may even say that it could have stood alone as a 'dialogue of refutation'. But these dialogues are serious, and surely not consciously unfair. And if it had been written and laid aside, Plato, when he came to take up again the problem of Justice, was not so poor that, if he did not think what he had already written adequate, he could not write something else by way of opening. We must, therefore, if we are puzzled and dissatisfied, believe nevertheless that Plato was content. Are we then to suppose that he was incapable of seeing how weak the arguments which he put into the mouth of Socrates were? Or are we dissatisfied with them

* From *Ancient and Modern Philosophy* by H. W. B. Joseph (Oxford, 1935), pp. 1–14. Reprinted by permission of the Clarendon Press, Oxford.

because we misunderstand them? Those who have read their Plato longest will, I think, be most inclined to the second alternative.

At any rate, I myself have come to believe that my original dissatisfaction was merely due to misunderstanding; that the discussion in this book is of great value both in itself, and in relation to what follows. And I should like to make an attempt to set forth the grounds for my belief.

The problem of the *Republic* may be said to be, how a man should live. Socrates himself gives that as the subject on which Thrasymachus and he are arguing. Now one way of settling that problem is by giving a list of duties; and many men, in many ages, live by such lists uncritically, or at least accept them as what they ought to live by. Yet sometimes they ask, Why these duties? and sometimes, Are there any duties? Is it not wise to please oneself, so far as one can, without regard to others?[1]

In the argument between Polemarchus and Socrates, Plato is dealing with the first of these questions; and he shows, indirectly, that the problem what a man should do cannot be settled by giving a list of duties. In the argument between Thrasymachus and Socrates, he is dealing with the second; and he shows that the implications of 'acting wisely' are inconsistent with such a rule of action being wise. The remainder of the dialogue develops and justifies these conclusions. We are given a picture of the organization of a perfect commonwealth and an account of the constitution of the human soul, in order that we may see how *what* any man ought to do depends on his nature and powers, and his place in the commonwealth of which he is a member; therefore it cannot be laid down in general rules. And we are given also an account of what wisdom is, that we may see how the very notion of living wisely, implied in asking how a man *should* live, involves distinguishing between what is really good and what seems so, and how to seek what is really good is to subordinate our chance desires.

This is, of course, a very summary statement, and only of the main outline. Some critics may object to it on the ground that Plato

---

[1] It may be objected that the second of these two questions is wrongly put; there are duties, and a man ought not merely to please himself; if 'Why not please oneself?' means 'Why ought I to do my duty?', the question is absurd; if it means 'Shall I do my duty, and not rather please myself?', this is not a question, but an expression of the thought involved in deciding. But to Plato it seemed that a wise man would endeavour to attain what is good, i.e. to make himself, or his soul, or his life good; and that what we ought to do is what contributes to this.

never does attempt to show that there is anything a man ought to do,
but merely what it is in his interest to do.[2] These critics, however, are
accusing Plato of mistaking one question for another, passing from one
to another without seeing the difference between them, not of explicitly denying that a man has any duties. As a statement therefore of
the outline plan of the *Republic*, and the relation of the first book to
the rest, what I have said may still be correct; I am not concerned here
with the justice of the critics' accusation. Of course there are many
points in the arguments of the first book which any so summary a
statement must ignore, many anticipations in it of later discussions that
connect it with the rest. Some of these will appear as we proceed. But
the above is the general thesis that I desire to justify.

We need not spend long over the first few pages, before Cephalus
retires, leaving the argument to Polemarchus; though we may notice
how there appears in them the subject of the life after death, and the
lots awaiting in it those who have lived justly or unjustly here, to
which the dialogue returns at its close; and also how in Cephalus himself we have a picture of a man living rightly of custom and without
understanding: a way of life which at the close is indicated not to be
sufficient, and with which indeed the effort of the whole dialogue
shows that Plato was not content. The conversation gives Socrates
opportunity to raise the question whether what justice is can be told
by giving a list of duties: 'this thing, justice, shall we say that it is
thus simply to speak truth, and to restore anything one may have taken
from another, or may these deeds themselves be sometimes justly done,
sometimes unjustly?'[3]

This question, or rather the wider question it implies, viz.
whether any list of duties can tell us what justice is, whether justice
can be defined by specifying the ἔργα δικαιοσύνης,[4] is handed over by
Cephalus to Polemarchus, and I have suggested that it is Plato's main
purpose, in the discussion which follows between him and Socrates, to
show that the answer is No. Incidentally we may remind ourselves
how in other dialogues Plato proceeds similarly, in the *Laches* with
courage, in the *Charmides* with temperance. Each virtue may be
thought to require of us its own definite acts; and yet there are shown
to be situations in which a man thus virtuous should act differently

---

[2] Cf. Prof. H. A. Prichard, *Duty and Interest*, pp. 5–21.
[3] i. 331 c 1.
[4] The phrase is from Xen. *Mem.* iv. ii. 12. The whole of §§ 1–20 there should
be compared with *Rep.* i. 331 e 1–334 b 7.

from how it seemed that the virtue in question would make him act. And for discriminating these situations knowledge is necessary: not any knowledge, but knowledge of good and evil. But what the relation of this knowledge is to all those different knowledges required for doing well the different kinds of action which a man has to do, remains a problem. The same problem is before us here. Plato would have us see that it is not co-ordinate with those specialized knowledges. The occasions for applying them exclude each other; the occasion which calls for the knowledge of a physician does not call for that of a sailor. But to act justly or rightly, to live as one should, needs some other sort of knowledge called for on all occasions and in which the requirements of all particular virtues are somehow comprehended. Of this knowledge two things may be said, that distinguish it from those specialized knowledges. It cannot be discriminated from them, as they can from one another, by assigning its particular field, specifying its ἔργα. And its possession is bound up, as theirs is not, with what we should call qualities of character, that may depend partly on nature, φύσις, but must be developed by a proper nurture, παιδεία. All this we are shown as the dialogue proceeds. What is sometimes called the Socratic paradox, that virtue is knowledge, probably never meant that the difference between a good and a bad man is a merely intellectual difference, like that between men who do and who do not understand economic theory. Certainly Plato in the *Republic* never teaches that. He does indeed teach that if a man really knew good and evil, he must ensue one and eschew the other; and that without knowledge, or in default of true opinion, about good and evil no man can live as he should. But that much every one must allow who is not prepared to accept 'What you think you ought to do' as a sufficient answer to the question 'What ought I to do?' or to the question 'What is good?', 'What you think good'. No doubt Plato denied that a man can deliberately reject what he thinks good; οὐδεὶς ἑκὼν ἀδικεῖ. But that is not to hold instruction enough to make any one a virtuous man, as it is enough to make him a doctor. The knowledge (Plato thought) required for living a good life is differed from that required for being a doctor, or for doing well any specialized work, in another way than merely by not being specialized; it involves the whole soul in a way in which they do not.

The argument with Polemarchus falls into two main parts, (*a*) from 331 d 4 to 334 b 9, (*b*) from there to 336 a 8. In the first it is shown that what justice requires of a man towards others is not restricted to any special occasions of his intercourse with them; in the second, that the 'others' towards whom it places him under obligation are not some men only. If justice then must inform his actions towards all persons on all occasions, clearly its nature and requirements cannot be shown by giving a list of duties.

But whereas (*b*) is a straightforward argument, reaching the conclusion which Socrates would have Polemarchus accept, (*a*) is indirect, proceeding by *reductio ad absurdum*. This may make the reader suppose that it is a piece of quibbling, in which Socrates merely entangles his opponent, without interest in the truth. But absurdity may be reached either by bad argument or by proceeding from false assumptions. Was Plato taken in by quibbles put into the mouth of Socrates that any freshman can detect? If not, and if he knew them for quibbles, why should he have introduced them? Is it not possible that the absurd conclusion is reached fairly from false assumptions which were clearer to him than they are at first sight to a modern reader?

I believe this to be so, and that the false assumptions are so many forms of a single error, that of supposing that the practice of justice (or righteousness) consists in the performance of specifiable acts. It is the error of those who believe in 'the righteousness which is of the law', and has been common enough at all times. The Pharisee who said 'I fast twice in the week; I give tithes of all that I possess' entertained it. But we are apt to think the error lies merely in overlooking the spirit in which the acts should be done. 'The letter killeth, but the spirit maketh alive.' This is not Plato's point, though he certainly did not think the spirit in which a man acted irrelevant, as may be seen notably in *Rep.* iv. 443 c 9–444 a 2. Polemarchus, in the passage we have to consider, imputes to a just man the purpose to help his friends; but so equally does Socrates. It is not by slipping in the unfair assumption that justice is a mere matter of skill without regard to purpose that Socrates develops his argument. There is another side of the error of the Pharisee which Plato would bring out. In whatever spirit a man may fast and give alms, when he has done that, he has not done all that is required of him. Or, to use the list of duties in our text, though he speak truth and pay what he owes out of love of his friends or because he thinks he ought, he need not be just; for sometimes justice requires that he should not act thus, and it requires very much besides.

We need not, therefore, charge Plato with letting Polemarchus confuse the statement that to pay one's debts is just with the definition that justice is to pay one's debts (331 d 2–e 4). For his case is more than that this definition incorrectly specifies the works of justice; it is that justice cannot be defined that way at all. Simonides, whom Polemarchus quotes, in support of the definition he takes over from his father, as saying that to pay one's debts is just, might have mentioned other acts, which, together with this, would have made up such a definition of justice; but the argument could proceed just in the same way from such definition as from the saying of Simonides.

For Socrates' first step is to show by instances (as he had already suggested to Cephalus) that sometimes a man ought not to restore to another what is owed to him; whereupon Polemarchus glosses the saying, and declares that I owe to another not what is his in the sense of a thing he had lodged with me, but good if he is a friend, and evil if he is an enemy (331 e 5–332 c 4). What is owing to any one is what is fitting. This is a much more elastic term, and indeed Samuel Clarke tried to find in the notion that what is right is what is fitting to the given situation, a means of showing that morality is a matter of demonstration. But he failed, because there are no principles from which we can deduce conclusions in detail about the conduct fitting on each occasion. And just as little can we set it out in lists, stating it without deducing it. If to treat a man justly is to treat him as is fitting, there is no intercourse of a man with others which is not an occasion for justice; a man may not sometimes practise justice and sometimes medicine, as he may sometimes practise medicine and sometimes seamanship.

But how then is practising justice related to practising medicine or seamanship? If justice is to be defined by naming its works, it will not serve to name the works of medicine or seamanship, for that would be to indicate not what a just man but what a doctor or a seaman does. Socrates, however, puts questions to Polemarchus which imply that justice is to be defined by naming its works, because Polemarchus has started from that position. We are not told that this assumption is the source of all the trouble. We are left to discover it.

Socrates takes the statement that justice is to render to each what is fitting, and shows that for rendering to certain subjects certain things fitting, a man is called a doctor or a cook. For rendering to what subjects what that is fitting is he to be called just? For doing good to friends and evil to enemies, replies Polemarchus. But is it in virtue of justice that he can do this? In what concerns their health and sickness the doctor is best able so to act; when they are at sea, the seaman. When and for what is it the just man who is best able to help his friends and harm his enemies (332 c 5–e 4)? Polemarchus should have refused to name any special occasions; but that would have been to abandon the assumption that governs his thought; and he replies, in fighting on their side or against them. But what when there is no fighting? A man's justice must be of use also in peace. Yet so are husbandry and shoemaking, for different purposes; for what is justice useful? Again he specifies a particular sort of purpose—in matters of contract. But a contract is an undertaking in which men engage together, and according to the nature of the undertaking different kinds of men will be useful. For what undertaking is it a just man that is required? For those concerning money, Polemarchus suggests; and again he ought to have suggested no special undertaking. For if money is to be used, as in buying or selling a horse or a boat, it is knowledge of horse-flesh or of boat-building or sailing that is required; and the question occurs once more, when is it justice that is required? Polemarchus replies, when money is to be deposited and kept safe; and no doubt it is highly important that those to whom money is entrusted should be honest. But if justice is required when money is to be kept in safety, not when it is to be used—and the same would apply to anything else, as well as to money—it will result that in the use of anything justice is useless, and useful only when anything is not in use (332 e 4–333 d 12). This, as Socrates observes, does not make justice a very fine thing; and he might have added that it brings Polemarchus back to the position from which he started, and which he had endeavoured to amend, that it is in virtue of his justice that a man restores what has been lodged with him. And Polemarchus has been driven back to it because at every turn he accepted from Socrates questions implying his own assumption that for the practise of justice, as for that of medicine or seamanship or any other art, there are special occasions.

It is often said that Plato makes false analogies between conduct and the arts. But if we read this book carefully we shall see that he thinks conduct in some ways differs from the arts, and in some shares their nature. It differs in not having, as every art has, a special field or subject-matter. It shares with them that it can be either right or wrong, correct or faulty. The part of the argument between Socrates and Polemarchus which we have so far considered is intended to bring out this difference. In the argument between Socrates and Thrasymachus, Plato endeavours to show what is involved for conduct by that which it shares with the arts. It is not accurate to say even there that he argues from the analogy of the arts. What he does is to make us see what a character acknowledged to be common to them and conduct involves in them, and to ask us to admit that this is involved for conduct also.

Since in carrying on any art, and also in conduct, a man may proceed correctly or faultily, rightly or wrongly, an art and conduct are so far the same. But if we went on to say that conduct is one of the arts, it should then, like them, have its special field or subject-matter; and justice, which is what a man's conduct should show, would be shown precisely in that field or subject-matter. But the consequence would be to exclude it from all action in which a man exercises any art commonly so called, for these arts are delimited from each other by having different fields or subject-matters. That is what Socrates has so far shown. If then there is an art of conduct, or of living, as in a sense Plato thinks there is, the practise of it must somehow coincide with or inform that of all the special arts. But how it can is no easy question.

Socrates now turns (333 e 6–334 b 6) to a fresh point, arising out of the conclusion that justice is of use merely to safeguard what is out of use. That conclusion is anyhow absurd, but it is to be shown so even more glaringly by this ensuing argument: one which is apt to arouse what I think is ill-considered hostility. On the assumptions so far made, however, it is a fair *reductio ad absurdum.*

He applies the principle, formulated later by Aristotle, that contraries fall under the same capacity. Those who can best deliver can best ward off a blow; those who can best guard against can best secretly convey disease, and so forth. If then the use of a just man were for safe-keeping, it should also be for circumventing the precautions of others to keep things safe; he will be able not only at guarding but at thieving, and so turn out to be a sort of thief—κλέπτης τις.

The obvious retort is that to possess a power is not to have the will to use it; that justice is a matter of character and purpose, not of skill. But Plato is not forgetting this. Ever since Polemarchus' statement to that effect at 332 d 5, it is assumed that a just man's purpose is to help his friends and harm his enemies. The question has been how precisely justice qualifies him to do this. In one situation seamanship, in another a knowledge of horse-flesh will do it, and so forth; and if justice has a restricted field, alternative to theirs as theirs are to each other, that field has been reduced to safeguarding what is not in use. Granted that his justice is such a special power which the just man possesses, and that he uses it to help his friends, if the same power enables him to circumvent others' safeguarding, why should he not use it that way to help his friends also? It is not suggested that he will steal for himself any more than that he will keep for himself what is lodged with him. That is why Socrates says he will be κλέπτης τις, a *sort* of thief; the common thief steals for himself. If justice, thought to be shown by a man in helping his friends and harming his enemies, is not to inform all that a man does, but is required only on special occasions, we naturally ask why those are the occasions on which it is required; presumably because on those occasions, and not on others, it is by justice that a man can help his friends or harm his enemies. If that is so, justice must be a specialized ability, which it is reasonable he should use for the purpose in question in all ways in which it admits of being used. And one way would be to steal (perhaps from their enemies) and give to one's friends. This consequence is, no doubt, absurd. But the moral is, that justice is not to inform a man's conduct only on special occasions, and so cannot be defined by any list of a just man's ἔργα or works.

We come now to (*b*) the second main part of the discussion, 334 c 1–336 a 8. This is not a *reductio ad absurdum*, but proceeds directly to a conclusion we are meant to accept. We have been shown indirectly that there is no restriction on the occasions when justice must inform a man's action; we are now to see that there is no restriction on the persons towards whom it places him under obligation. The formula that distinguishes the 'rendering of what is fit' which is justice from other 'rendering of what is fit' said that a just man should help his friends and harm his enemies; but this implies not so much that he has a duty to his enemies to harm them, as that he has no duties to them, and is therefore at liberty to show his manhood in their despite. The spirit in which he will act towards his enemies is that expressed in an oath which Aristotle tells us was taken in some oligarchies: 'I will be of evil mind towards the people and devise against them any ill I can.' Hitherto Socrates has developed the assumptions underlying Polemarchus' account of how a man's justice will manifest itself, so far as his purpose is to help his friends. Now he examines them so far as a man has to deal with those who are not his friends.

Socrates begins (334 c 1–335 a 10) by pointing out that to distinguish men as one's friends and enemies is not the same with distinguishing them as good and bad. It cannot be just for me to harm the good, who themselves do not act unjustly, merely because I happen to be at enmity with them. He assumes that any one would be on terms of friendship or of enmity with others according as they seem to him good or bad. This accords with the Socratic and Platonic conviction that at bottom every one desires what is good. But the assumption is not crucial to the argument. What is crucial is the admission that the formula about helping one's friends and harming one's enemies must be amended by saying that it is just to help one's friends when they are good men, and harm one's enemies when they are bad men. And Polemarchus admits this because he sees that justice requires of me to treat others according to what they are and on some principle, not according to my liking and capriciously.

But the question now arises whether it can be just to harm anybody: whether even their being bad men therefore can make it just for me to harm my enemies. Others besides Gomperz[5] have said that in this passage (335 b 2-e 5) Plato confuses two senses of the word βλάπτειν, to harm or injure. But the charge is unjustified. Socrates asks if a horse or a dog, if harmed, will not be made worse in respect of its specific excellence. This being granted, surely a man if harmed will be made worse in respect of a man's specific excellence, and that is justice. But it is impossible that by justice I should make others less just, for the spread of justice would then defeat itself. Gomperz thinks there is an undoubted confusion here between harming or injuring in the sense of rendering unserviceable and in the sense of causing pain or unhappiness. But Plato is not saying that to a man no more than to a horse or dog is it ever just to cause pain. Pain may be justly inflicted by way of punishment, but that would be for a man's benefit, and not to harm him. So pain may be used in the training of an animal and not harm it in respect of its specific excellence. But if you knock an animal about, because of its faults, venting on it your ill temper, you will make it worse. And if you treat bad men that way, they will become worse too. A merely vindictive (which is not the same as a retributory) penal system may be fortunate enough to have only bad men consigned to it; it will not be fortunate enough to make them better. The injunction or even the permission to 'harm' the bad means that one may treat them as having no rights; and a man treated as having no rights will be led to deny or disregard rights in others. A just man may treat others differently according as they are good or bad, as he may be entitled to treat differently in some respects his friends and his enemies. But the principle of justice does not permit that against any one he should devise whatever ill he can: no more against a bad man than against a personal enemy.

Justice then cannot be what Polemarchus thinks it. It is a principle that must inform all a man's actions towards all with whom he is brought into intercourse. What that involves, and how, while no definition of justice by naming its works is possible, we may yet give an

[5] *Greek Thinkers*, E.T., iii. 55-6.

elucidation of its nature that another sort of definition can enshrine, Plato endeavours to show in the long discussion from ii. 368 e 2 to the end of the fourth book. But in the remainder of Book i he examines a very different view. Polemarchus at any rate thought that, in distinguishing just acts from unjust, men acknowledged obligations that could conflict with their desires, rights in others no less than their own rights. Thrasymachus in effect rejects rights and obligations altogether. The only right is the right of the stronger, which in a moral sense is no right. The only obligation is that which Paley admits, 'a violent motive resulting from the command of another'[6]—a motive, that is, furnished by somebody who commands under penalty for disobedience some action contrary to one's inclination.

6 *Principles of Moral and Political Philosophy,* bk. ii, ch. ii.

THRASYMACHUS'
CONCEPTION
OF JUSTICE*

Ernest Barker

The first conception of justice which Plato seriously studies is one
which is enunciated by Thrasymachus, and which represents what
Plato understood to be the view entertained by the Sophists. Thrasymachus takes up two positions, and is successively driven from
both. Understanding by justice (what is understood throughout the
Republic) the standard and rule of action for a man living in a community,[1] he defines it first as "the interest of the stronger". In other
words, might is right; a man ought to do what he can do, and deserves
what he can get. This is to identify *jus* with *potentia*, after the manner of Spinoza; but while Spinoza somewhat inconsistently limits the
potentia of each individual by the *imperium* of a State, which enforces
a peace consisting in rational virtue, Thrasymachus logically enough
argues that the *imperium* of a State merely lays down as the law whatever is to its own interest, and simply makes into justice by its superior

---

* From *The Political Thought of Plato and Aristotle* by Ernest Barker
(New York, 1906), pp. 94–99.
    [1] It must be noted that no legal significance attaches to "justice" in Plato's
use of the word. We must not suppose for a moment any distinction of private
morality and public duty, or restrict justice to the latter. The two are one; and
justice is both. Justice is the standard of action to be observed, both by a man
acting as a member of a community, and by a number of men acting together as
a single community. It is thus the one standard for all human action; for in one of
these two ways men must always act. It is the answer to the simplest of questions—
What is it that I ought to try to do? There is no question of any difference between what I ought to do as a man upon my conscience, and what I ought to do
as a citizen under the law. I always am a citizen, and there is only one "ought".
Some distinction there is indeed in Plato, between justice as in one member of a
community, and justice as in all the members acting together as a community.
But this is a different distinction; and it is not one of principle. Justice whether in
one member (the individual) or all the members (the State), has the same essential nature, and it is only the scope of its action which is different. We must not
distinguish politics from ethics.

17

power the rights which it claims as the strongest. Accordingly, the standard of action for a man living in a community is, according to Thrasymachus, the will of a ruler who wills his own good; and this, he maintains, is what one must inevitably see, if one looks at the facts with an unblinking eye. For while every man acts for himself, and tries to get what he can, the strongest is surest to get what *he* wants; and as in a State the government is the strongest (or else it would not be the government), it will try to get, and it will get, whatever it wants for itself. Justice thus being whatever is for the ruler's interest, it follows that, for everybody other than the ruler, justice may really and in truth be defined, according to a popular definition, as "another's good". To be "just" is to be a means to the satisfaction of another: to be "unjust" is to act for the satisfaction of oneself. But the real standard of action for any sensible man is to satisfy himself; and therefore injustice and not justice is the real virtue and the true prudence. The wise man is he who will be just, and satisfy his ruler's selfish desires, *if he must;* but who, *if he can,* will be unjust, and satisfy his own.

Thus, in Plato's view, do quack theories turn black into white, and make the better argument appear the worse. There is a certain attraction in such theories. The view that the strongest individuality should dominate the rest is after all not unlike modern theories of the Overman, such as one finds in Nietzsche and even in the hero-worship of Carlyle. The whole position represents the revolt of an awakened self-consciousness against the traditional morality, in which it has hitherto passively acquiesced, but which it now brings to the bar of this new sense of self for judgment. The new sense of self is keen and urgent: it finds in traditional morality merely a number of limitations on its play; and in its young vigour it thrusts them aside, and claims room for free expression. With a fresh naïveté it enunciates its new doctrine: "I will do whatever I can, and seek whatever I like". Its cardinal error is the pettiness of its view of self, as an isolated thing to be fed with pleasure and fatted with power; and those who like Plato have to expose this error must answer by urging a true conception of the nature and the "rights" of human individuality. They must show that the self is no isolated unit, but part of an order with a "station" in that order, and that fulness of expression and true consciousness of pleasure are to be found in doing one's duty in the station to which one is called. And this is the ultimate answer which Plato gives, and writes the *Republic* in order to give. For the present, however, he satisfies himself with a logical refutation. He takes the two positions which are advanced by Thrasymachus—that a government governs for its own advantage, and that injustice is better than justice—and deals with them each in turn. To the former view he opposes the Socratic conception of government as an art. All arts, he argues, are called into existence by defects in the material with which they deal. The physician attempts to remedy the defects of the body; the teacher those of the mind. The aim and object of every art is the perfection of its material: the perfect teacher, for instance, is he who has remedied all the defects, and elicited all the possibilities, of his pupil's mind. And therefore the ruler, so far as he acts as a ruler, and in accordance with his art, is absolutely unselfish: his one aim is the welfare of the citizens who are committed to his care. As a man in need of subsistence—as one who pursues the art of earning a wage—he may indeed seek his own advantage, and earn a wage by the work of his office; but this he does not do as a ruler, or as practising the art of government, but as an earner of wages, and as one practising the art of wage-earning. This is Plato's answer to the first position of Thrasymachus; and to the second he answers by an argument, designed to prove that the just man is a wiser, a stronger, and a happier man than the unjust. He is wiser, because he sees the necessity of acknowledging a limit (πέρας) to his actions—in other words, because he does not blindly rush at every pleasure, but walks steadily along a definite line towards a definite object. Limit is not here used (it never was used by the Greeks) in the sense of a restraint, but in the sense of a guide. It means a principle imposed by reason, which, by narrowing the countless avenues of activity down to a single path, guides man along that path. Wiser, because he acknowledges such a principle, the just man is also stronger. Even if a number of men would fain be unjust, to get the strength for an unjust action they must be just: they must stand shoulder to shoulder, and act justly by one another. Wiser and stronger, in the strength of a principle which binds him to his fellows, the just man is also, last of all, the happier man. The argument by which Plato proves this last attribute of the just man is one of supreme importance. He starts from the position, which has just been proved, that the just man is wiser than the unjust. But because he is the wiser, he is also the better, since the wise man is also the good. Goodness, or excellence (ἀρετή), is therefore to be predicated of the just man. Now ἀρετή is a general quality, which may be defined as the ideal discharge of function;[2] for

---

[2] This conception of an ἔργον, of a final cause of action, is to be taken in connection with that of limit: the end of action is the limit. It implies ultimately a teleological conception of the world: if there are ends appointed for all kinds of action, the world must be a kingdom of ends culminating, as they did for Plato, in a single end—the Idea of the Good. The conception of virtue as excellence in the discharge of function, and the teleological view of the universe, are both inherited by Aristotle, and implied (or stated) in the *Politics*.

each and everything has a function—an end which no other thing can serve, or which no other thing can serve as well. Goodness is a quality which may be shown in the discharge of any function; and the very charioteer who wins a race may be said to have shown ἀρετή. If this quality be present, its possessor will discharge his function well; if it be absent, he cannot possibly do his work as well as it ought to be done. There are thus many ways of excellence, according to differences of function; and the excellence of the just man will be determined by the nature of his function. That function is the function of living; and the just man, who because he is just is possessed of excellence, will discharge this function well. In the full sense of the words he will "live well," and be happy; while the unjust man, destitute of such excellence, must needs live ill, and needs must be unhappy.

In these arguments there are implied deeper conceptions, which Plato ultimately unveils. The theory of justice as the force which gives coherence to any association of men, the theory of a special function for each thing, are theories which are developed to their full consequences in the later books of the *Republic*. But as they stand, these arguments are logical and eristic. They show us Plato playing with the Sophists at their game of words, and beating them at their own game. They are destructive, and not constructive: they tell us why we should not believe in Thrasymachus' view of justice; they do not tell us in what conception of justice we ought to believe. They have not indeed done away with the uneasy feeling, that though the frank brutality of the Sophist may be brushed aside, the fact remains, that justice is something to which human nature does not instinctively take, something as it were unnatural, and only present in man, because it has been put there by convention, and is kept there by force. This is the ordinary feeling of society: this is the tone manifest in public opinion. Accordingly Plato turns to the criticism of such public opinion; and, in order to show that justice is grounded in human nature—in order to show what it is, by proving it to be the natural order of the human soul—he leaves his logic for psychology, and deserts his analysis of terms for an analysis of human nature.

pointed? Eyes, he says, have a function, and they also have an *aretē*, excellence. The same for ears and all other things.

Here, at the start of his definition of *aretē*, Plato offers us a concise summary, as clearly and simply as it can be put in a general statement, of the traditional use of that term. *Aretē* always had a wide and flexible reference to anything that excelled in some activity; it is a word for skill and efficiency. It is a word that naturally would be taken to refer to a capacity or ability of some thing to do something superbly. In the *Meno*, Meno's attempts to define *aretē* reflect this association. Meno keeps speaking of an "ability"; his final attempt at definition is: *aretē* is "the power (*dynamis*) to obtain goods".[12] The relation of *aretē* and *dynamis* in Plato's present account remains to be explored. We shall return to it shortly.

The third stage of the argument now follows, with Socrates' warning to "pay attention".

Eyes could not perform their function well if they did not possess their own "specific excellence" and had in place of this a "defect". *Kakia*, which traditionally would mean 'cowardice' or 'wickedness', is now to be taken in the milder sense of 'defect', namely, a specific condition, the opposite of a specific *aretē*.[13] In general, then, of things with a function, by their specific excellence they function well and by their specific defect they function badly or defectively.

Such are the three steps of the argument before us. After this it is easy for Socrates to go on to maintain that since the human soul has a function it can also be said to have a special excellence and a special defect. Justice turns out to be the special excellence of soul, injustice

---

[12] *Meno* 78C.

[13] Concerning the terms κακία and κακῶς (badness and badly, defect and defectively) as Plato uses them here, it should be noted that two interpretations are developed and employed in the *Republic*: (*a*) *kakia* as the absence of a specific *aretē*—as such, a functional thing cannot perform its function well: (*b*) *kakia* as a power (*dynamis*) directing the bad or ill functioning of a thing. According to (*a*), *kakia* is the lack of the power of *aretē*; according to (*b*) it is a specific power and ability opposed to *aretē*. Both concepts are employed in different passages in the *Republic*. Thus the specific *aretē* (and *dynamis*) of the human soul is *dikē, dikaiosynē,* and *adikia,* injustice, is sometimes spoken of as the absence of this excellence, as in (*a*), sometimes as a contrary power or potency, as in (*b*), working to the badness or illness of soul. The two conceptions of *kakia* find their way into two versions of evil that derive from Plato in Western philosophy and theology: evil as the absence of good; evil as a force or power opposed to good.

The third part of the theory is stated at 353C: a thing "with its own specific *aretē* will perform its own function well, and by its defect, badly" (κακία δὲ κακῶς).

its special defect. Thus, functioning well of soul, which means living well, or well-being, requires the presence of justice in the soul. The unjust man cannot be said to have "well-being" or happiness, contrary to what Thrasymachus had claimed. The refutation of Thrasymachus follows easily, in part because the senses of "living well", "well-being" and "happiness" merge in a convenient and happy way for Socrates' argument.[14] But this happy result and the plausibility of it is not an issue of concern to us here. Rather in what follows, I wish to examine and comment on some novel and interesting aspects of this interesting and novel argument.

The passages we have just considered have the merit of providing us with a clear account of one significant way of specifying what is meant by *aretē*. Notice that this account of *aretē* is nested in the more general account of *function*. We can rightly call this Plato's "theory of function", the theory supplying us with the explanatory context for definitions of 'excellence' and 'defect'.

It is clearly not Plato's intention to propose that the function of a thing is what the thing in and of itself does. Thus it is the function of knives to cut and eyes to see, but the performance of a function will usually require the presence of agents who will initiate and make use of the function. *We* cut with knives, *we* see with eyes. We, or some kind of agent, will put the functional thing to work. Thus, confining our attention to human users of functions, we recognize that it is men who make use of functional things for various purposes. This is to be stressed, because the language of "purpose", "goals", "aims"— in short, teleology—while it may have a place in this theory of function, must not be misplaced. It is sometimes thought that we can treat phrases like 'the function of a horse' (or 'knife', or 'eye') as equivalent to 'the purpose of a horse' (or 'knife', or 'eye'). Two sorts of difficulties then result:

(1) We seem to be assigning to instruments, or organs, some animate or conscious trait, as if the objects called "functional" also possessed a desire to function. This might be a way of interpreting the language of Aristotle (i.e., *hormē*, drive or impulse) where he discusses matters closely resembling what Plato says about functions. But Plato does not even introduce the word *telos* in this theory. Nor does he

---

[14] That is, living-well, doing-well, well-being are conveyed by *happiness*, *eudaimonia*. Plato says (354A), the righteous man lives well (*eu zōn*) and is blessed (*makarios*) and happy (*eudaimōn*). And Aristotle explains: *eudaimonia* is usually understood to be the same thing as living-well (*eu zōn*) and doing-well (*eu prattein*) . . . *Nicomach. Ethics*, 1095a–20.

ascribe conscious purposes to functional things. He suggests but does not discuss the fact that it is with the user, not the functional object, that purposes are to be located. A word like 'purpose' can be misleading and ambiguous. We say a shuttle has a purpose, meaning here a use, not a conscious goal.

(2) Following from confusion over the first point, a frequent mistake is made in supposing that Plato invests the language of function with moral interests or with premisses for value judgements. On this view Plato has, so to speak, built into the theory of function devices enabling him or us to maintain that things with functions *ought* to function, that it is *good* for knives to cut, eyes to see. Here, too, this reading of Plato *might* be due to reading him through Aristotle. One result of this view was to achieve popularity later, especially in Stoicism: the universe was seen as a great system of things striving to function, working to achieve their respective purposes and ends; perfection of the whole was envisioned as the gradual completing of functions of the parts.

Now Plato does not surreptitiously introduce value terms into the theory. The powerful word *'agathos'* does not appear in the language of the theory at all. The terms 'better', 'best', 'superior', 'appropriate' do figure here. But these are to be taken in straightforward fashion as neutral terms replaceable by more detailed descriptions of functions. That is, Plato is saying, a knife is superior to, or better than, a chisel for whittling wood. The term 'better' carries no ethical import here. It simply provides, in context, an implicit reference to something that might be desired and the most efficient means to achieving that end. Thus 'a knife is better than a chisel' in this case is translatable: 'if someone wishes to whittle, a knife will serve more efficiently than a chisel'. The issue of efficiency and ease with which different objects can be used is settled by neutral appeal to neutral facts.

We might want to say: 'knives are good for cutting, and a good knife cuts well'. But we cannot derive from the theory the further, very different conclusion: 'it is good that knives can or do cut'. That conclusion, if it is to be derived at all, must come from a different sort of premiss. Elsewhere in the *Republic*, we know, Plato does speak of the Good as the "cause" of all things good, real, knowable, and true. In the *Timaeus* he tells us that the reason we have eyes and can see is that we will look at the stars, acquire ideas of motion, order and number, and hence become philosophical. Thus it might be said, if only by a philosopher, that it is good that eyes do function since blinking begets thinking. But all this lies outside what Plato does say in the theory of function.

Thus far we have not said anything about what *is*, undoubtedly, the ethical content of the theory. The theory does assert something about *aretē* and *kakia*, namely, that we should expect to find one of these terms applicable to anything with a function. We shall apply just one of these terms as a result of observation of the particular performance of a particular functional thing. If the performance goes well, we assign *aretē* to the object; if ill, we assign to the thing a defect (*kakia*). These value terms are relative to a standard of functioning for a class of functional things.

Much depends, of course, on specification of the standard for the good or ill functioning of things. It is at this point, though Plato does not discuss the consequences, that we are led to speak of "good" horses, knives, eyes, etc., meaning they satisfy in their respective ways the respective conditions of standards of functioning well. It is at this point, also, that we can detect two kinds of use of Plato's functional language, uses that I shall call "vacuous" and "filled-in". If we ask what is a good knife, for example, we are probably asking for a *specification* of the function of knives. A vacuous reply will consist in reiteration of the general formula of function thus: "a good knife is one that performs its function well". The use of 'good' here is something like the case we looked at above. In that neutral sense of 'better' in which it can be said "knives are better than chisels for whittling", we are now led to say "some knives are better than others for performing the knife-function". The words 'better' and 'good' here again simply refer to relative considerations of efficiency, ease, and effectiveness with which knives are used. Still our talk of the function of knives remains vacuous. To "fill in" such talk would be to specify in detail just these conditions of efficiency and effectiveness of use, to state not merely *that* some things function well or ill but *how* they function when they function well.

The vacuous application of functional language is not without all significance. For it may aid us in how and where we are to look for filled-in specifications of functions. If someone in doubt should wish to inquire as to what is meant by 'a good knife', he might be helped by the general vacuous formula that will advise him, to wit: (*a*) look to what knives alone can do or do best; (*b*) then look to those knives that perform just that sort of function efficiently. This is by no means a weighty answer to the initial inquiry. It is hardly an answer at all. But it does serve as preliminary instructions for how one is to start looking for an answer.

Now the vacuous use or formula does supply us here with an equally general (or vacuous) sense of *aretē*. We can state vacuously what the function of something is, and just as vacuously we can state that the *aretē* of a thing enables the thing to function well. But we should notice that, for Plato, the specific excellence *enables* the thing to function well.[15] This last feature introduces *dynamis* (power, ability). That feature comes out clearly in later parts of the *Republic*. Adeimantos wants to know what justice, the specific *aretē* of the soul, really *is;* he asks for a specification of its power in the soul. He is asking *how* this excellence, as a power, enables the soul to perform its functions well. He asks, then, for a filled-in use of the functional language. The vacuous use has been established; justice enables the soul to perform its function (of living) well. The request and challenge for Socrates is: provide us with a filled-in account of this function and excellence. The discussion of the model state, of the soul, indeed the rest of the *Republic*, is set forth as an answer to this question.

2. FUNCTIONAL LANGUAGE

I have been using the expression 'functional language' and 'functional terms' loosely, referring to the theory we have been considering. But it would be well, perhaps, to try to clarify some features of this language.

With certain possible exceptions, Plato is talking about *types* of things with types of *erga* (functions). We are to think of fairly well-populated classes here: all horses, all knives, every eye, every ear, and so on. Of each of the members of each class we affirm a function—and affirm also, therefore, a specific excellence or defect related to the performance of function.

While the word 'knife' applies to or denotes each and every knife, affirming the knife-function will be true, presumably, of just the same objects. (There may be trouble here in assigning functions to non-existent or mythical objects, say Achilles' knife, but let us pass

---

[15] As a *dynamis*, the specific excellence is a necessary condition for a thing performing its function well. The *dynamis* does not, however, produce the functioning of any object. Thus sharpness is necessary to the knife performing its function of cutting excellently. But the sharpness of blade does not produce the operation of cutting. Both Plato and Aristotle seem agreed on this; a *dynamis* is a necessary but not sufficient condition of the performance or work of a thing. But, contrary to a scholastic interpretation of Aristotle, for any thing to be put to work, to *do* something, requires (in Aristotle's language) an efficient cause; and *dynameis* are not efficient causes.

over this question.) 'Knife' is a word, but knives are not, nor is the knife-function. The latter is what every knife does better than any other class of things. We might suppose that non-vacuous statements of functions will in general serve as definitional descriptions of various sorts of functional things. By speaking of 'definitional descriptions' I merely mean that in stating what is the function of horses, knives, eyes, etc., we are not only supplying information about these objects (say, that knives can cut), but that the description is to be regarded as a statement of the necessary and sufficient conditions for something to be a horse, a knife, an eye, etc. This is to suppose, then, that knowing what a knife is and knowing its function are the same.

Now this proposed extension of Plato's comments about function, or something like it, has, I suppose, been the motivating insight behind such comments from writers on Plato as that "the function or *ergon* of a thing is its being; you cannot separate the two ideas. If you are asked what anything is, every answer you give describes a function of the thing".[16] Knowing the function, it would seem, is knowing the "being" of a thing. Certain objections, reminiscent of the worst temper of scholastic disputations, are bound to arise at this point, pressing for a ghostly—even ghastly—revival. What of the dull or broken knife—is it still a knife despite its lost function? The ancient retorts come flocking at this recall: "a broken knife is not a knife" goes one, not shirking the patent contradiction in speaking of a knife that is not a knife. We remember the advice of Epictetus: When your wife dies, why be distressed? She is no longer your wife or a wife at all, for she has lost her function. Another familiar retort is: "a broken knife is a knife in name only". This is interesting for its ambiguous suggestion that a once-functional thing, by loss of function, becomes a name; but it is on the right track in also suggesting that we can continue to call the once-functional knife a knife.

Instead of stoutly refusing to call a broken knife "knife", thereby being rendered speechless when confronted with once-functional objects, and reluctant to coin new names for them (or pool them in new classes), thereby encumbering our language—we compromise. We simply draw upon the stock of available terms adequate for the purpose, like 'broken knife', 'bad knife', 'useless knife'. Knives that are

---

16 R. L. Nettleship, *Lectures on the Republic of Plato* (London, 1901), p. 230. Note the departure in the above from Plato's argument. A thing for Plato has one function. Nettleship may have been guided by the famous pronouncement in the *Sophist* (247E) reading it as Plato's own doctrine. There it is suggested that the *real* is power (not *ergon*, but *dynamis*).

knives in name only, knives that are not "really" knives, knives that would be knives if they could function, knives that are no longer knives are each and all very odd entities. Aristotle would call these *equivocal uses* of the word 'knife', allowing us to speak of knives that are not knives. Rightly, he would not permit equivocal uses of names to blind us into supposing the existence of equivocal entities. Ockham's razor would threaten these entities too, lest we go on to consider how a once-functional knife differs from a once-functional eye. How is a knife that is not a knife different from an eye that is not an eye? These are refugees of Ockham's barber shop.

But let us observe what our strategy commits us to doing. Suppose we affirm as a general rule R1:

The name 'knife' names just those things of which the non-vacuous statement (or definitional-description) of the function of knives is true.

If we find it strategic, nonetheless, to speak of broken knives, or useless ones, we have relaxed our allegiance to R1. Once-functional knives, blind eyes, and the like can be regarded as respectable objects capable of respectable linguistic reference. But we enjoy this advantage only at the expense of departures from the functional approach (and rules like R1) from which we began.

Knowledge of what a knife is is not quite the same as knowing the functions of knives; the statement of function is not quite a definitional description, the statement of function is not quite a statement of the necessary and sufficient conditions for something to be a knife. The "not-quite" clause here points to an area over which our strategy advises us of the departures from R1 of the sort noted, just those cases where we do and will wink at principles like R1 while otherwise swearing loyalty. There are advantages, as well, in keeping departures from rules like R1 at a minimum. We want, if we use the language of function, to have settled non-vacuous statements of function with fairly sharp application to clearly discernible classes of objects. Border-line cases, such as broken knives, cause trouble if there is no relaxing of principle. But too much relaxing, like too many borderline cases (or exceptions to the principle) means a diminishing return in the use and informative value of the principle. This tug-of-war over comparative but differing dictates of strategy in the use of language is, however, seemingly inevitable—reducible but never wholly eliminated.

These observations help explain, I think, the source of many apparent "metaphysical" problems, when functional language is used. A notorious case is the Aristotelian functionally-oriented remark "it is the nature of acorns to become oaks". The old questions arise again: what of acorns that do not become oaks? Are they acorns, or are these acorns not acorns? More acorns are eaten by squirrels than become oaks. Why not, then, say that it is the nature of acorns to become squirrels? Acorns that do not do what comes "naturally" may indeed go the way of squirrel food, children's games, and ammunition for sling shots. If, in the Aristotelian pronouncement on the nature of acorns, 'nature' is construed as *function* (in the sense of §1) then the acorn that does not become an oak is in the same company of metaphysical errants as broken knives or blind eyes, the anomalous objects remarked above. Shall we call them acorns or not? Are they acorns (in that accommodating phrase noted earlier) in name only?[17]

These questions derive from several kinds of indecision as to which of several divergent advantages of functional language (or its uses) we want most to enjoy. Thus, interested in knowing something about acorns—even in evolving an empirical theory about them—we may be led, along with Aristotle, to view them as potential oaks. We shall say that it is the function of acorns to become oaks. We may offer vacuous statements of this function or we may progress to filled-in ones and hence to a definitional description of acorns. We shall then have articulated why and how it is that acorns become oaks. This is to advance from a statement that something has a function to explaining how it functions. In all this, no umbrage need be taken at the fact that some acorns do not become oaks. Indeed, empirical theory is extendable, perhaps, to account for the deviant exceptions or the spectacle of popular alternative careers for acorns. To say of acorns that it is their function to become oaks can be informative.

But another interest, quite as legitimate as this last, will, when it manifests itself, take a different direction. This is the interest in how 'acorn' is used in functional language; it is a concern with 'acorn' as used in the theory of function and not directly a concern with the function of acorns. Here, something like R1 might be invoked:

'Acorn' is true of those objects whose function it is to become oaks. This, too, is informative, but this time the burden of information is more upon the use of 'acorn' than about acorns. It is here, also, that

---

[17] Thus see Aristotle, *De Partibus Animalium* I, Ch. 1: 640b–641a:

A hand formed in any and every manner, out of bronze or wood, is not a hand except in name, any more than a flute carved in stone can perform the function of a flute. . . . Likewise the eye or the hand or any other part of a corpse is not really an eye or a hand.

For this passage and a discussion of the point above in context of Aristotle's own "functional theory", see J. H. Randall, Jr., *Aristotle* (New York, 1960), pp. 233–35.

the medley of familiar strategic devices commences. Acorns that do not become oaks are "not real", they are "apparent" or simply not acorns, or they subsist as unrealized and errant acorns, or their function subsists despite their failure to perform, etc. The exceptions to this application of R1 for acorns get disposed of by ruling them "apparent" exceptions or ruling them out altogether by definition.

We need not at this point go on to the re-telling of an old story. How once upon a time there were statements about the world and how, later, some of these underwent an adventurous change into definitions or acquired an analytical status. Rather, one observation is suggested as a result of what we have been seeing thus far. What ordinarily passes for the difference between analytic and synthetic statements in ordinary language (ignoring for the present the current dispute over this distinction) resembles the distinction I have drawn above between "vacuous" and "filled-in" statements of function. In Western philosophy the use of functional language, encouraged and stimulated by Plato's theory of function, has been a favourite *genre* of metaphysics. We have seen how metaphysical and evaluative issues will proliferate even over the simple occurrence of an acorn becoming oakless. Some, though not all, of this proliferation is rooted in the confusion of various differing interests and uses afforded by the language and theory of function, differences just discussed. The chief source of the confusion lies in passing, without notice, from talking about the functions of things to talking about how our talk of these functions is best made economical, unambiguous, and informative. To revert to the original mention of R1 in the light of the difficulties previously surveyed, it is just the too rigid adherence to rules like R1 for using the language of function that breeds much bad metaphysics. Such rigidity counsels, for example, treating broken knives as not knives, acorns that do not become oaks as not "really" acorns. The rigidity results in incapacitating the language of function for dealing with the borderline cases discussed. What were once empirically informative statements get strait-jacketed into definitional truths of little or questionable usefulness. Bad metaphysics thrives on semantic confusion.

We have looked at Plato's theory of function and at some of its conceptual and linguistic features. In what follows I propose to depart from the foregoing expository considerations and to reflect on some more general consequences of Plato's theory as they have bearing on some other characteristic aspects of his thought. This is not to sever all connections with what has been said; it is merely to move from the *what* of the theory to the *so what*, the one making the other possible.

3. FUNCTION, KNOWING, AND FORMS

Despite some difficulties already touched on as to the claim that knowledge of a thing is knowledge of its function, the general theory of function does lead us to some basic issues in Plato's conception of knowledge. A famous comment of Aristotle's informs us that Socrates concerned himself with ethical subjects, "seeking the universal (or general, τὸ καθόλου) in these matters" and directing attention to definitions.[18] In the early dialogues this is how Plato represents the Socratic quest. The search for definitions is a search for a representative type or standard instance of what is being defined. This is a search for Forms, but not for transcendent Forms.

In the *Euthyphro* Socrates considers the question what piety is. If we are to define it, or state what it is, we must concentrate not just on any instance of piety but on a representative type or standard case. This case will be the Form (*eidos*) of piety; and Socrates speaks here of the "look" (or the shape, *eidos*) of piety itself.[19] In some passages of the *Republic*, Forms are spoken of in this sense; in others, they are described as transcendent entities.

The language of Forms in this first sense, as about standard observable instances of phenomena—or about natural kinds of things— is drawn from uses in Greek medicine and mathematics. There, the terms for Form (*eidos* and *idea*) are almost invariably bound up with the term *dynamis*. The medical writers speak of Forms or types of elements and symptoms and their powers; the mathematicians speak of Forms or types of numbers and their powers (often meaning roots).[20] Understanding a subject consists in getting at the Forms and powers. Much of that language is retained in Plato.

Now the language of function plays a rôle here. For we have seen briefly that *dynamis* and function have a significant connection. It is *dynamis* that enables a thing to perform its function. Without *dynamis* the thing cannot perform; and if the *dynamis* is the special excellence of a functional thing, it *enables* the thing to perform well.

Thus the Socratic quest for definitions comes close to being represented as a quest for non-vacuous statements of function or for

---

18 *Metaphysics* 987b.
19 *Euthyphro* 6D: . . . ἐκεῖνο αὐτό τὸ εἶδος . . .
20 This remark about Plato's use of *eidos* and *dynamis* and, in the second paragraph that follows, the comment on *psychē* and *polis* are treated in some detail in the present writer's forthcoming book on the *Republic*.

definitional descriptions of functions. Socrates could ask what *kind* (*eidos, idea*) of thing piety or justice is. But we can represent this question *via* the theory of function as follows. Excellences are powers (abilities, *dynameis*) enabling functional things to do their function well. To ask what is *justice* is to ask for a filled-in account of the kind of function that those things perform well with this power (with *dikē, dikaiosynē*). And this, as we noticed, is precisely what Plato proceeds to do in the *Republic*.[21] First and foremost, it is *psychē* and, secondarily, a *polis* whose function is performed well with the possession of this *dynamis*. Much of the dialogue is a filling-in or specifying of this function and the specific excellence and their connection.

We already noticed how statements of functions are akin to definitions. The topic of definitions, in Plato, naturally prompts us to think of Forms. If statements of the Form of a thing are statements of what the thing *is*, this passes for definition—an all too familiar theme in discussions about Plato. We need merely note here how talk of function and Form can overlap in this respect. Asking what is the *eidos* is much like asking what is the *ergon*, at least insofar as we confine our talk to functional things. Perhaps this was the source of the claim that the *ergon* is the *being* of a thing.

Along these lines, if we consider the supreme locus of value, the Good, the approach *via ergon* is as informative as that of *eidos*. Socrates speaks of the Form of the Good ("Goodness itself") but is not prepared to define the Good or to discuss it in detail. The explanation we do receive, though deliberately metaphorical, takes a functional turn. The Good is said to be a "cause" (*aitia*) and "power" (*dynamis*), the source of all being, truth, and intelligibility. Plato's words, brief and eloquent on this highest principle in his philosophy, depict the *function* of the Good—what it alone can do and does best.

4. THE FUNCTION OF LANGUAGE

There is another way in which the notion of function plays a significant rôle in Plato's thought. This is, as it were, the converse of

21 Notice as remarked earlier (last paragraph of §1), that the fundamental theme of the *Republic*, raised as the question for inquiry in Bk. II, is stated this way (358B): concerning justice and injustice, says Glaucon, I want to hear what each of them really is, and what *dynamis* each has in itself, within the soul. . . . Again (366E–367E) it is asked: what does the dynamis of justice (*dikē, dikaiosynē*) and injustice *do;* what is the inherent effect of each in the soul, or in the one who possesses them?

what we have hitherto been considering; it has to do not with the language of function but with the function of language.

It is well known that Plato lays down the following rule concerning statements (*logoi*): statements are composed of two necessary units; without at least one of these joined with the other, a statement cannot result. One of these components Plato calls *rhēma* (usually translated 'verb'); the other unit is *onoma* (translated 'name' or 'noun'). Statements, says Plato, "are a combination of *rhēmata* and *onomata*".[22] The passages from which this analysis is culled (the most informative on *statements* being the *Sophist*) are brief and vague. Plato appears to have taken for granted what earlier grammarians had said about these matters, though we must recall that a science of grammar was a post-Platonic development. Furthermore, the grammatical terms 'verb' and 'noun' bear only a rough correspondence to the terms Plato uses in his remarks about statement composition.

Overlooking more precise distinctions between singular and general terms in statements,[23] Plato proceeds to say that the *rhēma* (the verb-like term) is "an expression which is applied to actions". The *onoma* (the noun, or proper-name-like term) is "a spoken sign applied to what performs these actions".[24] He points out that a series of the verb-like terms or a series of the proper-name-like terms will not alone suffice to make a statement. By a *statement* Plato seems to mean an assertion, true or false, about "things that are" or existent facts. The two sorts of *words* that compose statements are treated as names of "being" or of "existing things".[25] Roughly, then, statements contain at least two components, both names, one the name of an action, the other the name of an agent (or object) who performs the action. Plato's comments foreshadow the traditional analysis of statements into subject and predicate and the analysis of the referents of statements into substance and attribute.

In spirit, if not in fact,[26] Plato's view of statement composition comes to this: in a statement one of the words (the *onoma*) names just one object whose presence or location is tacitly understood in the

[22] *Cratylus* 431B: *Sophist* 261E.

[23] Examples of *onomata* that Plato gives are 'lion', 'stag', 'horse' (*Sophist* 262B). Also 'a man' and 'Theaetetus'. As names these differ, some naming one and only one object ('Theaetetus'), others naming many ('lion'). The *rhēmata*, we shall see, are also to be construed as names of many objects (or "actions").

[24] *Sophist* 262A. Trans. Cornford in *Plato's Theory of Knowledge* (1935).

[25] *Sophist* 261E.

[26] Cf. the confusion over singular and general terms noted above.

utterance of that name; the other word (or words, the *rhēmata*) does not ordinarily name one thing, but many. Thus, Plato's example, "Theaetetus is sitting" names Theaetetus and names an action. The latter name 'sitting' is a name of any case of sitting *and* a name of the Form, Sitting.[27] The action term, *rhēma*, it should be noticed, is given a wide latitude. Let us keep in mind, then, that 'actions' has a very large sense: among the names of actions, Plato includes such words as 'wise', 'tall', 'white', as well as more obvious action words like 'sitting' or 'walking'.

But we are concerned with *function* and not with the whole of Plato's philosophy of language. Thus it is the *rhēma*, the kind of word that names actions, that is of special interest to us here. For clearly, it is this term which, while being a name for any action, will also be a name of a function.

A study of how Plato describes the two components of statements will show that one description is derived from the other. The *rhēma*, we have seen, names actions. But the description of *onoma* goes: "what performs these actions". *Onomata* then are described by reference to *rhēmata*. It is like saying: "a proper name is a name of that which *does* what is named by a verb". The burden of explanation rests on what is meant by a verb.

The emphasis given to *rhēma* here as the primary term in the analysis of statement composition is faintly like the emphasis placed upon *actions* (in the large sense of 'action' noted above) in the analysis of our knowledge of things for Plato and Aristotle. This is more than saying that "by their actions ye shall know them", to which in general Plato, Aristotle, and Pragmatists subscribe. For Plato, most, if not all, *rhēmata*, names of actions, have a predicative or attributive rôle in statements. This term is singularly important in speaking, just as the corresponding action is important in knowing. For this is the term that expresses what the agent or object is *doing* (once more, in the large sense of action[28]). *Rhēma* words are the vehicles of classification, analysis, and description of the agent or object. So it is by means of these words that speech can yield two results: (1) We are able to name an existing fact true of some object, as well as the Form of which the

---

[27] This is Plato's "same name" principle, often employed in his accounts of the Forms. The Forms, he says, have the same name as the particulars participating in them. Thus, 'sitting' or 'to sit' names a particular act and also names the Form Sit (or Sitting).

[28] Through action words we can express what the agent is *like*, where, when, and how he and his parts are what they are, etc.

existing fact is an instance or participant. For as we saw in 'Theaetetus sits', the *rhēma* term 'sits' names an existing action true of Theaetetus if sitting, and the same term names a Form, Sitting, of which the action of Theaetetus is an "instance" or "participant"; (2) By means of some *rhēmata*, we can express functions as, e.g., in saying the function of the eye is 'to see' or 'seeing'. For Plato, knowledge is of Forms or of functions. But knowledge of anything, insofar as "things" can be known, involves interpretation of the existent facts (i.e., "actions") true of some object. And, for Plato, *interpretation* is of facts as "instances" of Forms or functions. The *rhēma* terms are the linguistic instruments for expressing truths (or falsehoods) and communicating knowledge.

The *Sophist* and *Cratylus* reveal Plato's conviction that there is a vital link between language and the world. There is the suggestion, which time and again has proved of fascination to philosophers, of a language evolved from a set of simple and primitive names—these being the names of the most simple and ultimate constituents of the world. Plato considers several of these languages and several ways in which the use and structure of statements has a relation to the structure of nature and Being. All this is not to be wondered at if we look at things through Plato's eyes, for language, too, is a part of nature and a reflection of Being.

In the *Cratylus* Plato discusses the difference between descriptive proper names (like 'Hermogenes' = 'of the race of Hermes') and names established by convention (*nomos*) that name but do not describe the "nature" of the thing named (like 'Plato').[29] It is affirmed several times that "things" (*pragmata*) have a fixed being (*ousia*) of their own; and the same is true of actions (*praxeis*).[30] Talk about things, if it is to be significant and supply information, will have to be guided by and respondent to the fixed character of things (their *physis* and *eidos*).[31] If we are to succeed in any art, or in knowing, we cannot proceed in any indiscriminate and haphazard fashion or use just any instrument. Now language, says Plato, is also an instrument (*organon*),[32] and speech is a kind of action (*praxis*) concerned with things.[33] Thus the correct construction and use of language (or

[29] The example may be unfortunate for the name also happens to mean fat or bulky.

[30] Cf., e.g., 386E.

[31] 390E.

[32] 388A.

[33] 387B–C.

names)[34] requires the guidance coming from knowledge of the natures or the character of things. The carpenter makes or repairs a shuttle. He looks to the essential character (*eidos*) and tries to embody this in each particular work (*ergon*).[35] But the weaver *uses* the shuttle; he possesses knowledge of whether this shuttle is a good instrument or not. In knowing the use (really the function) of the shuttle, he knows whether this work of the carpenter is good.[36]

For Plato, then, language is a functional thing, an instrument. What is its *ergon*? The vacuous reply would go: the function of language is what it alone can do or do best. But filled-in, this means as Plato says: language is an instrument for conveying information about and making distinctions concerning reality (*ousia*).[37] A language that functions well will be supervised in its construction by the man who knows its function. If language is to be able to express the "nature" (*physis*) and Forms of things, it is the dialectician, Plato's philosophic hero, who guides its construction, for he is the true user of language.[38]

The ideal of a scientific language shaped by scientific users can be glimpsed behind the complicated and diffuse course of argument in the *Cratylus*. But we need not try to follow any further here. For we have found that according to Plato, the test of language and of its excellence is the degree to which Forms and functions are efficiently and conveniently expressible in it. To find this much is all we are looking for: it is to find the language of function at work in Plato's analysis of the function of language.

[34] Here *onomata* are treated as descriptive names or descriptions.
[35] 389B–C.
[36] 390B.
[37] 388B–C. This is said of names, *onomata*, but *using* (descriptive) names seems to be what is meant.
[38] 390D–E.

PLATO'S APOLOGY:
*REPUBLIC I**

Alexander Sesonske

It is at this point, I believe, that Plato's thought takes a different direction from the philosophy of his master, Socrates. There are two ways in which a man may approach the task of conceiving an ideal society. One is to start with the moral reformation of the individual, and then to imagine a society consisting of perfect individuals. This is the logical outcome of Socrates' mission to his fellow-citizens as described in the *Apology*. The other is to take individual human nature as we find it, and to construct a social order that will make the best of it as it is and as it seems likely to remain. This is the course taken by Plato in the *Republic*.[1]

Thus F. M. Cornford, in his essay "Plato's Commonwealth," identifies the juncture at which Plato's method diverges from that of Socrates. It is not, of course, a minor divergence. From its source in the freedom exercised and cherished by Socrates who, feeling that "each person must organize his own independent search for the good,"[2] would discuss any question with any man who would ask and answer, Plato's path leads toward that scene imagined by Cornford as a counterpart to Dostoyevsky's "Grand Inquisitor" in which Socrates, arraigned for a second trial before the Nocturnal Council of the *Laws*, is confronted by Plato in the president's chair.[3] Nor can we accept the implication that this divergence is lightly undertaken by Plato. We cannot reasonably either simply denounce Plato's betrayal of Socrates, with Popper, or pretend that the Platonic drift away from Socratic modes of thought and discourse developed so gradually that Plato himself was unaware of it.

If any writer still accessible to us can be said to have known and

* From *Phronesis*, VI (1961), pp. 29–36. Reprinted by permission of the editors of *Phronesis*.

[1] F. M. Cornford, *The Unwritten Philosophy and Other Essays* (Cambridge: Cambridge University Press, 1950), pp. 58–59.

[2] Bruno Snell, *The Discovery of the Mind* (Cambridge: Harvard University Press, 1953), p. 180.

[3] Cornford, op. cit., p. 67.

understood Socrates, it is surely Plato—we must admit this if only
because *our* Socrates is so completely a product of Plato's art. And if
there is one aspect of Plato's relation to Socrates of which we may be
certain it is Plato's belief in the injustice of the trial and death of his
master. The whole series of dialogues in which Plato recreated the
life and character of Socrates is testimony to this; the simple assertion
which concludes the *Phaedo,* "Of all the men of his time whom we
have known, he was the wisest and justest and best," is Plato's summa-
tion of that life. It is apparent also that Plato long adhered to what
were for him the basic Socratic insights: the connection of knowledge
and action, and the belief that true knowledge could not be *given* to
one person by another—fed out of a spoon, as Thrasymachus suggests
in *Republic* I (Cornford's translation)—but rather must be drawn out
from within by dialectic, a process of question and answer.

Yet, if we acknowledge that the account of the activities, the
'mission', of Socrates given in the *Apology* is authentic and also maintain with Plato Socrates' innocence of any guilt, we must see, as Plato
saw, that the Socratic method had failed. The men, young and old,
who had listened to Socrates and responded to his questions were
not—certainly were not all—made wise and virtuous by him; he did
not corrupt them, but neither did he save them from corruption.
Alcibiades, Charmides, Critias are perhaps the most obvious examples
to cite here, though if one agrees with Plato's modern enemies the
name of Plato himself might perhaps head the list of those who were
most attentive to Socrates and were not made better by the experience. As Cornford claims,[4] Socrates may have used 'eristic' only to
expose the pretensions of sophists and others who claimed superior
wisdom and who could not be convinced by argument; it must also
seem that Socrates failed in competing with these pretenders for the
mind and soul of Athens. Should we not perhaps concede the accuracy
of Callicles' statement, "Somehow or other your words, Socrates,
always appear to me to be good words, and yet, like the rest of the
world, I am not quite convinced by them."[5] And, remembering with
Plato the trial and death of Socrates, should we perhaps not find a
note of Platonic irony in Socrates' claim to be the only living Athenian
who practices the art of statesmanship after denying that title to
Pericles, Themistocles, *et al.,* on the ground that they had been tried

---

[4] F. M. Cornford, *Before and After Socrates* (Cambridge: Cambridge
University Press, 1960), p. 45.
[5] *Gorgias,* 513.

or exiled by the people and therefore could not have made them better? If not irony, certainly an awareness that, though a statesman, Socrates was an unsuccessful one.

If the Socratic method of question and answer provides the correct avenue to knowledge and virtue, and yet does not lead there for most of those who respond to the sting of the gadfly, then it must be either that not all men are capable of real knowledge or that adverse circumstances prevent the method's effective use. Though correct, the method may not work for everyone and under adverse circumstances may perhaps not work for anyone. Plato's turn away from Socrates involves an admission of both of these alternatives. There are indications of this in several dialogues, but in the first book of the *Republic* Plato most clearly acknowledges Socrates' failure and displays the reasons for it, thus justifying his departure from Socrates in the remainder of the dialogue. It is in this sense that *Republic I* may be called Plato's apology. In trying to sustain this view I shall not discuss the arguments of Book I—there is ample literature on those already; but I shall focus upon the dramatic framework by which Plato gives point to these arguments.

Legend has it that Plato rewrote the opening section of the *Republic* ten times. If this is true, or even if it isn't, it is surprising that few commentators have seen fit to allow any significance to the initial scene of the dialogue. The conversation with Cephalus presents some of the themes and anticipates some of the results of later portions of the work; this much is admitted. But the opening sequence is generally treated as a prologue having only dramatic interest. A recent exception to this rule is the discussion by Eric Voegelin[6] of the first nine lines, and particularly of the first word, κατέβην, which Voegelin sees as opening "the vista into the symbolism of depth and descent". By identifying the Piraeus with Hades he connects this prelude with the descent to Hades in the myth of Er and, by inversion, with the ascent from the cave. Voegelin's remarks increase our awareness of the unity of the Republic and show how the opening lines function in creating this unity, but he does not discuss the role of this section within Book I, nor its relation to the transition which occurs in Book II.

"I went down to the Piraeus yesterday with Glaucon, the son of Ariston, to make my prayers to the goddess." The speaker is Socrates, the man who was put to death after being accused of introducing new

----

[6] Eric Voegelin, *Order and History, vol. III: Plato and Aristotle* (Baton Rouge: Louisiana State University Press, 1957), pp. 52 ff.

gods in Athens. Here we see him acting, as perhaps he did, like an ordinary Athenian. But the words he speaks are not his; they are Plato's. As such they prompt us to ask, who is Bendis and what is she doing in Athens; and to see, perhaps, that the answer, which Plato gives, not only reminds us ironically of Socrates' death, but also illuminates the failure of his mission.

Plato tells us this about the Bendidea: this was the first celebration of the festival. The Thracians made as fine a showing in the procession as our own people. There is to be a torch-race on horseback, which is something new. There will be a festival lasting all night which will be worth seeing. We shall find plenty of young men there.

When we bring these remarks together we see, not only Plato's irony, but also the corrupted Athens which put Socrates to death. Imperial, cosmopolitan Athens attracts all things, trade, gold, itinerant professors and wandering goddesses—and welcomes them all. The Athenians not only admit the Thracian goddess, they throng to her festival. And they have become so adept at putting on the new that one must remark (with wonder?) that the Thracians, to whom after all the goddess belongs, made as fine a showing as did the Athenians. All the young men are there, including Glaucon and Adeimantus, whom we must surely accept as representing here serious young men of good character and family, honestly seeking a way of life.

But though all the young men welcome the new goddess, we need not wonder why Meletus does not bring a charge against the Thracians. They have indeed given Athens a new divinity, but a most accommodating one who will make no real difference at all to the religious life of the community. All that she demands is that they enjoy the spectacle. Is it not this which stirs Plato most profoundly? The festival from which the discussion of justice and the ideal state emerges is pure spectacle and entertainment, "something new," "worth seeing." Socrates' "crime" is not that he brought new divinities to Athens; we see here that this excites no enmity. His offence is the much more dangerous one of claiming that religion should be a serious affair. "Look to the gods for guidance in your actions. And if they speak to you, or in you, heed their words even though it may discomfit the state," such is the model presented by Socrates. In a society in which religion has become entertainment and spectacle, few are likely to imitate this model. We know both from history and from Plato that few did.

Between the first and the last of these descriptions of the Bendidea Plato constructs the brief scene in which he makes perhaps the major point of this opening sequence, a point which reverberates through the whole of the *Republic*.[7] Polemarchus sends a slave to catch Socrates as he turns back towards Athens and this interplay ensues:

> Socrates, said Polemarchus, I do believe you are starting back to town and leaving us.
> You have guessed right, I answered.
> Well, he said, you see what a large party we are?
> I do.
> Unless you are more than a match for us, then, you must stay here.
> Isn't there another alternative? said I; we might convince you that you must let us go.
> How will you convince us, if we refuse to listen?
> We cannot, said Glaucon.
> Well, we shall refuse; make up your minds to that.[8]

It is customary to dismiss these lines as mere by-play, with at most a simple reference to Polemarchus' "playful threat"[9] or "urgent invitation".[10] But though the threat may be playful Plato's point in recording it is surely serious. Here at the very outset of the discussion of justice we are brought up against the fundamental fact which any deep concern with justice must face. Socrates will argue cleverly against Thrasymachus' assertion of the doctrine that might is right, but before the argument occurs Plato subtly confronts us with the brute, or brutal, fact which gives that doctrine its force—the simple fact that might is *might*. Superior strength, if exerted, will prevail. We have here no dalliance with that illusion often evoked in such circumstances, the illusion that *since* we are right we shall prevail, the illusion that right is might. The fact of Socrates' death is enough to dispel that illusion, if Plato ever entertained it. Might is might, if exerted it will prevail—what, then, can we do? "Isn't there another alternative? We might convince you that you must let us go." The countervailing agent to might is reason, persuasion. Through the influence of reason might may be allied with right. Reason may persuade necessity, as Plato will say in the *Timaeus*.

But here again Plato confronts us with a brute fact: "How will you convince us if we refuse to listen?" Persuasion, or reason, can be

---

[7] It may not be too far-fetched to suggest also that the scene epitomizes the life of Socrates—it is in brief the story of his life.
[8] Cornford's translation.
[9] T. Gomperz, *Greek Thinkers* (London: John Murray, 1905), v. 3, p. 54.
[10] E. Voegelin, op. cit., p. 52.

effective only if all parties are reasonable, or agree to listen to reason.

We have here, in a moment, the world in which the Socratic mission must fail. Religion provides not a guide to action, but entertainment; men in power refuse to listen to reason. It is against this background that Socrates speaks with Cephalus about old age and the value of wealth, and disputes with Polemarchus and Thrasymachus about justice. No subject merits our concern more than this: "how to determine the whole course of conduct which every one of us must follow to get the best out of life." Socrates pursues the subject with persistence and skill, insisting as always that his respondents know what they mean and mean what they say. His method, in *Republic I* as throughout the early dialogues, is to seek truth via refutation; to elicit an opinion and then confront it with a contrary opinion held with equal firmness. It is a method requiring great logical agility whose exercise is based upon the faith that conviction and truth are to be achieved by finding in each respondent the true voice of his true self. To do this the many divergent voices (opinions) of the self must be made manifest so that the true one may emerge from beneath the welter of confused opinions. If a man will sincerely assert the beliefs upon which he is willing to act and then persevere with Socrates in the patient examination of them, the confrontation of one belief with another—never allowing a step to be taken in the argument unless he fully assents to it—the outcome should be a belief that is consistent and fully understood and one which has the same direct relation to action as did the first sincerely asserted belief.

Two thousand years later Descartes will found modern philosophy upon a conviction that one can proceed step-by-step from an intuitively certain truth to other truths which will be equally certain. The Socratic dialectic never begins with an intuitive certainty; truth may be the object of the inquiry but it is not built in at the outset as it would be in the Cartesian construction. Nevertheless Socrates and Descartes share the faith that the essential characteristic of the first premise in an argument may be transmitted without dilution through a step-by-step logical development, however long. But for Socrates the essential characteristic of all the oral arguments which he pursues is not truth but *conviction;* the conviction which welds belief to action It is perhaps this faith which is at the root of Socrates' assurance that virtue is knowledge.

The early dialogues of Plato portray the persistence with which Socrates adhered to this faith—and document its failure. The men, young and old, to whom Socrates brings his mission usually mean what they say at the outset of the discussion; they begin with sincere assertions of their convictions. And Socrates insistently solicits agreement for every step of the developing argument. But somehow, unaccountably, conviction drains off along the way. Socrates sometimes brings his respondents to confusion, sometimes renders them speechless, even makes Thrasymachus blush; but he does not change their actions or their lives. This failure may be sensed frequently; it is openly stated by Alcibiades in the *Symposium* (216) and by Callicles in the remark quoted above: "Somehow or other your words, Socrates, always appear to me to be good words, and yet, like the rest of the world, I am not quite convinced by them." They cannot question the argument; yet conviction has escaped. On both of these occasions an excuse for the failure is given: both Alcibiades and Callicles listen to Socrates and are moved by his words, but they reject the pursuit of knowledge and virtue because of their love of popularity and power, of Demus. But if true, is this explanation consistent with the Socratic faith?

The climax of Plato's documentation of this failure occurs in *Republic I*, immediately before Plato abandons Socrates' method and, in *Republic II*, begins to develop his alternative. The view of justice asserted by Thrasymachus resembles that championed by Callicles and, perhaps, lived by Alcibiades. Like them Thrasymachus is reduced to nodding assent as Socrates drives home his refutation; like them he is unconvinced. But his expression of his lack of conviction is strikingly different. As Thrasymachus' last statement in *Republic I*, it carries us back to the opening paragraphs and places the whole of the preceding argument once again in the context of that scene: "Well, he replied, this is a feast day and you may take all this as your share of the entertainment."

This line, like the opening scene, is generally ignored by commentators. But let it begin to reverberate in your ear and it is devastating. Though rejecting the Socratic way both Alcibiades and Callicles took it seriously, and their seriousness suggests the possibility of conversion. But with Thrasymachus' thrust the whole Socratic enterprise is brought to the level at which religion functions in *Republic I*—a spectacle, an entertainment. Both the equestrian pyrotechnics of the Bendidea and the logical pyrotechnics of Socrates serve only to amuse! What greater defeat can the Socratic mission suffer? Perhaps we may notice here that Glaucon and Adeimantus are also unconvinced; it is they who revive the argument in *Republic II*.

Here we should recall some words from the opening scene: "How will you convince us if we refuse to listen?" This is the crux of Socrates' failure. There are many ways in which one may refuse to listen besides using force to assure silence—the method by which Athens ultimately refused to listen further to Socrates. One way to refuse to listen is to be unable to comprehend even though the words are heard; another is to be always attuned to the plaudits of the crowd so that the Socratic voice must be filtered through the hubbub of Demus, and so never clearly apprehended. Another way is to allow the words to be spoken, and attend to them, but to treat the whole process as a game, a mode of entertainment, and thus drain the words of all significant meaning. If one reads the early dialogues in the light of this passage I think he will find examples of all these ways of refusing to listen. Their conjunction spells the doom of Socrates' mission. It also renders any question of the logical soundness of Socrates' arguments irrelevant.

Plato's departure from the Socratic path in *Republic II* is not a betrayal. Plato remains true to the Socratic insights: dialectic is the way to knowledge; knowledge issues in action. But though dialectic is the way to knowledge *it leads there only for those who are able to listen.* No one can listen who is unable to comprehend, who is a lover of Demus, or who comes only seeking pleasure, entertainment. Athens had not listened. Plato diverges from Socrates to begin to construct a world in which those who can comprehend will listen; a world in which reason persuades might to act in the service of right. The necessity for the divergence had by then been demonstrated.

STATEMENT OF
THE PROBLEM OF
THE *REPUBLIC**

Richard Lewis Nettleship

☆

At the end of Book I, Plato himself gives us a criticism upon it. He makes Socrates confess that in one way the result of the argument is nothing, because we have not settled what justice is, and cannot therefore determine whether it is a virtue and whether it makes men happy. We have been discussing the concomitant circumstances of the thing without knowing what it is in itself.

If we ask what the discussion has done, we may say that it has shown several things which justice cannot be; that various leading conceptions, those, for example, of art, wisdom, function, interest, have been analyzed; and further that it has been shown that the theory of Thrasymachus in its naked form will not account for the facts—that consistent and thoroughgoing selfishness will not give one a working principle of life at all. But Glaucon and Adeimantus feel that, though Thrasymachus has been silenced, the argument is not convincing. They undertake to renew his contention, and they demand an answer quite different from that which has so far been given. They want, as Glaucon says, to be shown what justice and injustice are in themselves, as powers in the soul of man; or, as Adeimantus says, not merely to have it logically proved that justice is better than injustice, but to be shown the actual effects of each upon the possessor. This is the question to which the last sections of Book I have led.

In passing then from Book I to Book II, we pass from the region of logic, and from an analysis of terms in which all depends on their being used precisely and consistently, to the region of psychology and to the analysis of concrete human nature (an analysis which leads

---

* From *Lectures on the Republic of Plato* by Richard Lewis Nettleship (New York, 1901), pp. 47–66. Taken from notes of lectures given 1885–88.

Plato to construct an imaginary community upon the basis of his psychology). We pass at the same time from the consideration of utterances of individual experience, borrowed and half-understood maxims, and paradoxes of cynical rhetoricians, to criticism of the voice of society and public opinion, as it speaks through its recognized leaders or in the everyday intercourse of social and family life. To notice one more feature of the transition from Book I to Book II, we pass from a Socrates represented as knowing nothing, but simply listening, questioning, and refuting, to a Socrates represented as the exponent of a new and higher morality.

The two personages through whom this transition is made, Glaucon and Adeimantus, are of a type that Plato takes an interest in representing. They cannot be better described than in the words of Adeimantus himself, where he speaks of 'young men of the day, who are gifted (εὐφυεῖς), and able to flit over the surface of public opinion and draw inferences from it' as to the true principle of life (365 A). They are greatly interested in speculation, convinced in their hearts that justice is better than injustice, but unable to defend their conviction against the voice of public opinion in its various manifestations; they are dissatisfied with the modern enlightenment, but cannot see where the real flaw in it lies, and how it should be corrected. . . .

Both are puzzled by the apparent incongruity between morality itself and the external circumstances amid which it exists, between the being of things and the seeming, the externals of life which all seem to point one way, and the principles which, they are themselves convinced, point the other way. The literature of all peoples shows that this has always been one of the first problems to strike the human mind.

Glaucon begins with a classification of good things, based on the distinction of things good in themselves and things good for their ulterior results. He and Adeimantus are persuaded that justice is good in itself and for its results, but to realize the intrinsic good of justice they wish to have it examined absolutely apart from its results; . . . Accordingly Glaucon requires that the distinction between justice and injustice should be represented in the most naked way. He will have justice on one side, and on the other side he will have put all the material results of justice that can be separated from it. Strip justice bare, he says; set against it all the good things that may often go with it but are not connected with it really, and may equally result from being thought just when one really is unjust; and then, convince me that this bare principle, with nothing to show for itself except itself, is better worth living for than everything that can be set against it.

This is the view which both young men wish Socrates to maintain. They themselves, for the sake of putting before him something to answer, give expression to views opposed to it, current views, which are not their own but which they have a difficulty in withstanding.

First, Glaucon represents the view which troubles him most. It is that morality is indeed a good thing, but is only good because it secures certain external results; it is not the 'natural good' (the best thing), but a compromise between a greater good and a greater evil; the greater good is to obtain the same external rewards without justice, the greater evil is to suffer the retribution of injustice. There are three distinct points in Glaucon's representation of this view. First (358 E to 359 B), he gives a theory of the origin of justice, explaining the nature of justice by showing how it arose. Secondly (359 B to 360 D), he maintains that justice is only pursued by men as a second-best thing, and not naturally but against their real desire; if we dared, he says, we should all be unjust. Thirdly (360 E to 362 C), he argues that in this the general feeling of mankind is reasonable, because if we look at the facts we see that all the advantages of life are on the side of injustice, or at any rate may be if the unjust man is clever. The conclusion is this: it is at any rate a possibility that you might have to choose between, on the one side, all the powers and all the material advantages of life, and on the other side the naked principle of justice. In that case, can you say that justice is the better of the two? And if you do say so, then what do you understand by 'good'?

Adeimantus gives expression to two different beliefs. The first (362 D to 363 E) is one which externally seems the direct opposite of that described by Glaucon, but which really tends to the same practical results. It says, Be just; for justice pays best in this world and the next; on the whole, the just man prospers. It says, Honesty is the best policy, and it says nothing more. It does not add, If you can be immoral with impunity, so much the better. Thus it is widely different from Glaucon's position; and yet, like Glaucon's, it resolves justice into the seeking of external rewards. And therefore it leads, as Adeimantus points out, to the same conclusion, namely that the really valuable thing is the reputation of justice and not justice itself. This, he says, is the view which is inculcated in ordinary education and in family life. The second view he expresses (363 E to 365 A) is this: Justice is in itself the best thing in the world, but injustice is much pleasanter, and, if proper steps be taken, can be made to secure as satisfactory results; for, to go to the root of the matter, the gods are not just themselves, but can be bought over with the fruits of injustice. This is the most thorough-going demolition of justice, for it asserts that the divine nature, its fountain-head, can be corrupted.

The passage in which these various beliefs are expressed has a great incidental interest for us from the light that it throws on certain opinions current at that time about religion, political right, and law. First, as we have seen, Glaucon gives us a popular theory of the nature of justice, explaining it by its historical origin. This is the earliest written statement that we have of a theory which has ever since played a great part in the world, the theory that moral obligations have their origin (whether wholly or in part) in contract (ξυνθήκη). This theory can be and has been applied in the most opposite interests and in defence of the most opposite positions. As Glaucon states it, and as we here have to deal with it, it is simply this: In the nature of things to do injustice is best, but men have found by experience that they cannot do it with impunity, and the greatest evil is to suffer injustice without power of retaliation. Men have therefore compromised the matter by making laws and institutions which save them from the worst evil, but do not secure them the greatest good.

The conception of an original contract upon which society is based is, emphatically, unhistorical . . . but it has not the less been influential. It is one of the most striking examples of the reflexion of an idea into the past to give it apparent solidity and concreteness. In this respect it is like the beliefs about a golden age which reflect into the past an ideal which men carry about with them for the present. . . . It is based upon a very important fact, that every civilized community, perhaps any real community, requires, in order that it may exist at all, a mutual recognition of rights on the part of its members, which is a tacit contract. It becomes unhistorical if one goes on to say that at a certain period in the world's history people met together and said, Let us come to an understanding, and make a society on the basis of contract. This has never taken place, but the potency of the idea lies not in the fictitious historical account it gives of the matter, but in the real present truth which it expresses.

As has been remarked, this idea has been used in the most diverse interests. It was applied by Hobbes to justify absolute monarchy, and by Rousseau to prove the absolute authority of the will of the people. It is easy to see how it lends itself to such opposite applications. On the one hand it may be said, Members of a civilized community have contracted themselves out of certain original rights, and the existence of the community depends on the maintenance of that contract; there-fore a strong government, or at any rate the maintenance of some government, is necessary, and nothing can be allowed to violate existing law. On the other hand it may equally well be said, The present government depends only on tacit contract, and the people who entered into this contract are at liberty to dissolve it whenever they think fit. As Glaucon here applies it, the theory is used destructively and in a revolutionary interest, to show that justice is a matter of contract and convention *only;* and there is further a most important implication that all convention, and therefore all law, is a sort of artificial violence done to human nature.

The antithesis of nature (φύσις) and law or convention (νόμος), which thus lies at the root of Glaucon's argument, is one which was widely current in Plato's time. Like many other antitheses, it has different meanings in different people's mouths, and it generally owes its effectiveness to the fact of having no definite meaning but confusing different views. . . . And in the various uses of the antithesis we can generally trace a contrast between that which is radical and underived and that which is acquired, or between that which is permanent and universal and that which changes with circumstances. But no word is more ambiguous than nature; and in applying the formula to human action and feeling, some theorists have held that what is 'natural' in man is what he has most in common with the rest of the animal world; some, at the opposite extreme, think (as Plato and Aristotle emphatically did) that human nature is properly that in man which most distinguishes him from the rest of the animal world, the 'differentia' of man, not his 'genus.'

In one sense everything that man does is natural to him, law, morality, science, as much as anything else; his nature is all that he does. When this antithesis between law and nature is made, the antithesis is, so to say, within man. What then, it may be asked, remembering all the time that we are within human nature, is the ground upon which certain products of human nature are distinguished as natural, and others as conventional? In the antithesis as it is here used 'conventional' appears to stand for that which depends for its existence upon certain mutual understandings which society necessarily employs. Now, to speak of these as conventional is to recognize the truth that the existence of society does in the last resort depend on a mutual understanding; all the institutions of the state and of society are forms of mutual understanding, and, as they are emphatically creations of man, there is no reason why he should not dispense with them if he wished. If the theory of contract is understood in this sense, it is not profitable to dismiss it by saying it is unhistorical. That does not invalidate the fact, for it is a fact, that society is based upon contract. And we may go on to say with equal truth that the existence of society implies that the individual members of it agree to sacrifice a part of their individuality, or to sacrifice a part of their rights, if we call what a man *can* do his rights. Two people cannot live and work together without surrendering something which they would do if separate, for joint action is not the same as separate action. But is there any point in representing the results of this mutual understanding not only as conventional but as *merely* conventional, contrasting them with something natural which has a deeper authority? What is this something natural? What would man be naturally, in this sense of the word? The only answer to the question is that he would be himself *minus* everything that he is by convention, and that means *minus* everything in him which the existence of society implies. Such a 'natural' man does not exist, but that is the way in which we should have to think of him.

It appears, then, that while we may, in a true sense, describe laws and institutions as 'conventional,' it does not follow that they are therefore, in any true sense, contrary to 'nature'; and that there is all the difference in the world between saying that the institutions of society are based on compact, and saying that therefore they are unnatural or merely conventional. How is it, then, that the antithesis between natural and conventional is so common and has such a strong hold on us, and what do we mean by 'conventional' when we use the word, as we commonly do, with a bad signification? When we say an institution or custom is merely conventional, what we really mean is that it has no right to exist, because it has ceased to have the use which it once had. A law which has ceased to have any justification for its existence is the best instance of what people have in mind when they employ this antithesis. And the reason why there are endless debates as to what is merely conventional and what is not, is simply that people have very different ideas as to when the real occasion for a law or custom or institution has ceased to exist.

While then Glaucon's theory, by which justice is set down as a something conventional and contrary to nature, contains the great truth that laws and customs would not exist but for a mutual understanding, it ignores the significance of this mutual understanding. For not only is this understanding the work of man, it is what man in society has deliberately judged to be best. How has this deliberate judgment come to be passed? If it were true that to commit injustice with impunity is the real nature of man, there would have been no force to create society. The strongest motives are those which impel to action; and it would be impossible to account for the existence of society at all, if injustice had a special claim to be called the natural tendency of human action.

Glaucon, in the second place, goes on to contend that, as a matter of fact, justice is always observed unwillingly; that is to say, that morality, public and private, is only maintained by force. Here again a very real and important fact is made the basis of a very false theory. The existence of society does imply force, which is exercised in various ways. In every civilized community the established order of things is ultimately backed by the force of the police and the army. There are a certain number of people who can only be kept from injuring society by force, and the law of the land can only exist if there is physical force in the background. But it is quite another thing to say that force and the fear of force, in that sense of the word, is what maintains morality in the community; and it would be easy to show that, if the morality of a community really depended on force and on fear in the usual sense, it could not possibly continue to exist. You may, however, use 'force' in a quite general sense to include not only the police and army but the force of public opinion, the force of principles, ideas, conscience, and so on. These agencies are rightly called forces. They make themselves felt in very different ways in different individual cases; the force of society acts on a criminal by physical compulsion, and acts in quite a different way on a well-conducted citizen. But in these very various ways there is great force acting upon the component elements of society; and that is the truth at the basis of Glaucon's argument here. What is untrue is that society, in obeying its own laws, is acting against its own will. As soon as society begins to obey its laws unwillingly, their abolition is only a question of time. The most thoroughgoing despotism in the world never existed on a basis of mere force. If it be said that everybody would break the laws if he dared, the answer is that if that were true, everybody would dare; there would be no force sufficient to frighten him from it. This does not in the least exclude the fact that a large number of the members of society do obey the law from fear, and that a large number do not obey it at all.

To complete his theory Glaucon, in the third place, undertakes to show that this inward protest of the members of society against the supposed compulsion exercised by law is a natural and justifiable feeling, because the advantages of life are all on the side of injustice. There is no impossibility, he argues, in imagining all the advantages of life to be secured by the mere appearance of justice without the reality;

while the reality of justice might well exist without a single element of good fortune. This supposition is put by Glaucon in a very violent way in order to press home the question, If there is such a possibility as this in life, in what does the real advantage of justice consist? It may be said that what he describes is not altogether possible; the appearances and the reality of justice cannot be kept separate throughout every part of life; the consistently unjust man must somewhere drop the appearance of justice, and the man who consistently maintains the appearance cannot always escape the reality. But even if the picture is overdrawn, it brings out a very real difficulty, a difficulty which we cannot get away from so long as we measure the advantage of moral goodness by anything other than itself. As a matter of fact, the world is so ordered that there is no necesary correspondence between moral good and the material elements of prosperity; and so long as people expect to see such a correspondence, so long as they regard material prosperity as the proper result of goodness, they will be perpetually liable to have their theory of the world upset by facts.

We now pass to Adeimantus. The first view that he represents contradicts expressly that which is represented by Glaucon, but it brings out more clearly the same point that Glaucon had made, namely that the preachers of morality have always in one way or another confused it with its material results, though immoral consequences do not always follow from this teaching. Glaucon ends by showing that it is quite a possible supposition that the just should be miserable and the unjust happy; Adeimantus' first position may be briefly stated thus: justice secures happiness; therefore it should be pursued. This, he says, is the view of parents and of teachers generally. A certain prosperity, separable from goodness itself, is alleged to be the natural concomitant of goodness. Such a view is a natural distortion of a feeling in human nature that justice should have its reward. There is a kind of instinctive demand in the human mind that there should be some reward for good living, that life should be reasonable, that it should approve itself to us as just. The idea that God blesses the just man is expressed in all early literature, and notably in the Old Testament. It has nothing in it prejudicial to high morality, till in later times the principle that men are in some way better for virtue, is interpreted to mean that good men have a right to material prosperity, and material success thus comes to be made the criterion of goodness. In early times the idea is merely the readiest way of expressing belief in the righteous government of the world, but as a reasoned theory of later times it provokes the retort that good men do not always prosper.

This general idea of morality as connected with reward is extended by Adeimantus into a future life. The Eleusinian Mysteries have, he says, been agencies in increasing the expectation of reward in a future life for goodness in this life, and—for this is the point of the passage—this expectation of reward is made the motive of a good life. There is a great difference between saying that the soul is immortal and that it is better for it always to be good, which is the burden of the *Republic*, and saying that certain moral actions should be done for the sake of obtaining certain other desirable things.

The second view to which Adeimantus gives utterance is the natural counterpart of the first. It is one that is in vogue in private conversation, but poets and prosewriters may also be found expressing it. It dwells on the hardship and troublesomeness of the path of justice, and on the readiness of the gods to prosper the wicked and neglect the good. What the poets sometimes say of the indifference of the gods to justice in this life is reinforced by prophets and dealers in Mysteries. These teach expressly that sacrifices and prayers and ceremonies of initiation win the favour of the gods, for this life and the next, better than justice does. The complaint of the poets and the teaching of these prophets follow naturally from the tendency to identify goodness with material prosperity, or to make material prosperity the criterion of real success in life. There are abundant expressions in Greek literature of this belief in the injustice of Providence. . . .

In the concluding part of his speech Adeimantus sums up what is common to the views which he and Glaucon have put forward. They all depend upon the one belief that justice and injustice are to be sought or avoided, not for their own sake, but for the sake of something else. He proceeds to put in a vivid way the difficulty in which men like himself and Glaucon find themselves. They see the whole of public opinion arrayed upon the side of this belief; and, further, the burden of most that they hear is that with skill and by proper devices we may commit injustice, without forfeiting the material rewards of justice. As for the gods, either there are none at all, or, if there are, we only know of them through the poets, and these poets all represent them as open to corruption. In the face of this almost irresistible mass of public opinion what is there to keep a man from injustice except weakness and want of spirit? He can only be saved from it in two ways—by some divine grace or inspiration which gives him an instinctive repulsion from injustice, or by his somehow coming to understand its nature better than it is generally understood now.

The cause of this difficulty is that no one has yet adequately explained what are the intrinsic good and evil which justice and injustice, whether seen or unseen, have in them. This is what Socrates is now called upon to explain, dismissing for the present all consideration of the results to which justice and injustice lead through the impression they produce on others (δόξα).

JUSTICE
IN THE
*REPUBLIC**

H. A. Prichard

We are now in a position to consider Plato's treatment of justice, i.e. of the acts which form our duties, in the *Republic*. In Plato, corresponding to 'good' and 'a good to us', there is the use of ἀγαθός (good) as an adjective and of its neuter ἀγαθόν as a substantival phrase. By the adjective ἀγαθός he, of course, means good, as when he speaks of a man or a city as good, and maintains that there is a better and a worse element in the soul. And by the substantival phrase ἀγαθόν he must be admitted to mean not something good but what we mean by 'a good to us', i.e. something which excites pleasure in us whether directly or indirectly. The admission is inevitable for various reasons; but two considerations may be mentioned as decisive. The first is that in Plato ἀγαθόν means ἀγαθόν τινι, a good to *someone*, as in the statement put into the mouth of Thrasymachus that just action is ἀλλότριον ἀγαθόν τῷ ὄντι, τοῦ κρείττονός τε καὶ ἄρχοντος συμφέρον, οἰκεία δὲ τοῦ πειθομένου τε καὶ ὑπηρετοῦντος βλάβη,[1] i.e. is a good to another, being advantageous to the stronger and the ruler but being loss to the agent.

The second consideration concerns what is ostensibly a division of ἀγαθά (goods) but is really a division of objects of desire, at the beginning of the second Book. There he divides the things which we desire into three classes:

1. things which we desire for themselves and not for the sake of their consequences, such as rejoicing and harmless pleasures,
2. things which we desire both for themselves and for the sake of their consequences, such as intelligent activity, seeing, and being healthy,

*From *Moral Obligation* by H. A. Prichard (Oxford, 1949), pp. 103–111. Reprinted by permission of the Clarendon Press, Oxford. Originally published in 1937.
[1] *Rep.* 343 *c.*

3. things which we desire only for the sake of their consequences, such as gymnastic training, receiving medical treatment, and practising medicine.

These he represents respectively as (1) goods in themselves, (2) goods both in themselves and on account of their consequences, and (3) goods on account of their consequences. And since in referring to these as ἀγαθά, i.e. as goods, he cannot possibly be meaning that they are objects of desire, and so just stating in other words that we desire them, the only meaning which it is possible to attach to ἀγαθά is that of 'goods to us', i.e. things which directly or indirectly excite pleasure in us, these being divided into three kinds according as they excite pleasure directly, indirectly, or in both ways. No doubt this interpretation requires us to allow that Plato is involved in holding that we only desire anything so far as we think it will excite pleasure directly or indirectly. But this cannot be helped.

It is now possible to state Plato's treatment of justice. His first task is to state as strongly as possible the case against thinking that it is just rather than unjust action which is profitable. He represents the Sophists as presenting the case in two forms, in both of which just action is held—with, of course, some plausibility—to consist in carrying out the laws of the state, i.e. obeying the orders of the government. In its *more* superficial form, put into the mouth of Thrasymachus, the government is held to consist of a ruler who has successfully devised the laws in his own interest, so that it is the ruler who gains by just action, and the agent suffers whatever evil is incurred by conferring the benefit in question on the ruler. And Socrates is made to refute this view by an argument which even on its own lines, although showing that 'the ruler does not gain', does nothing to disprove what *prima facie* is the truth, viz. that by obeying the law, e.g. by refraining from stealing, it is not the agent but another subject who gains. In its *less* superficial form, put into the mouth of Glaucon, the case put forward is more complicated. According to Glaucon, men originally pursued their own interest regardless of that of others. But they found that they lost more by others acting regardless of any interest other than their own, than they gained by acting thus themselves. In consequence they mutually agreed to abstain from gaining at the expense of others, and to set up a government to order and enforce this abstinence. And a government having been thus set up, justice consists in refraining from gaining at the expense of others in a state thus set up, and so a state where this abstinence is ordered and enforced. Hence for most men it is not a good, but only a lesser evil than unjust action—being a lesser evil because the loss incurred by doing what is just is a lesser evil than suffering the penalty for doing what is unjust; but for those men—and there are such—who are either strong enough or skilful enough to avoid the penalties, just action is an evil, and unjust action a good.

In addition, Glaucon is made to strengthen the case in the following way. He is made to say that if Socrates is to show that the man who does what is just is necessarily happier than he who does what is unjust, he must succeed in taking into account both the case of the completely successful unjust man, who by his skill manages to obtain the advantages of a reputation for complete justice as well as those of his injustice, and also that of the completely just man, who in spite of his justice has the reputation for the greatest injustice, and so not only fails to gain the advantages of his justice but also suffers the penalties which attach to injustice. And though the reason for this which Glaucon is made to offer is irrelevant, viz. that otherwise the just man may be considered to be doing what is just for the sake of its rewards, he should have been made to offer a good reason, viz. that such a case is possible.

Finally, Glaucon is made to state what, in view of the case to be met, is the only possible method of meeting it, if it can be met. According to him, since all the rewards normally open to a just man are equally open to an unjust man, and since a just man may suffer all the penalties which normally go to unjust action, just action can only be shown to bring happiness by ignoring rewards altogether, and by showing that just action is *in itself* a good so great as to outweigh any possible combination of resulting evils.

Plato certainly did not underrate his task. Indeed, in reading his statement of it, we wonder how he ever came to think that he could execute it.

To carry it out he naturally thinks that he has first to get the right answer to the question 'What is justice?', i.e. 'What is the character common to the acts which are just or those which it is our duty to do?' And ostensibly he proceeds thus: He first considers what he represents as only an analogy to the just action in individual men, viz. the just action of members of an ideal community, and finds it to consist in each of what he finds to be the three parts of the community (the rulers, their subordinates, and the artisans) contributing that service to the community for which the special nature of each is best suited. Then, turning to the individual man, he finds that he also has three parts, viz. the intellectual, the spirited, and the concupiscent, and that his just action, and so justice proper, consists in each part doing in the interest of the individual that for which its special nature is best suited. And finally he urges that once we have realized this it becomes ludicrous even to ask whether a man gains by just action.

Yet this can only ostensibly be his procedure. For, in spite of what he says, he must be implying that his 'justice in the state' is identical with and not only analogous to his 'justice in the individual', and he must be going too far when he asserts that justice must really concern the internal and not the external performance of a man's proper work.[2] For the just actions, the profitableness of which his speakers are considering, are certain acts of a man to others, and unless he holds that the activity within the soul, which he maintains that just action consists in, shows itself outwardly in these acts, his argument is broken-backed. For otherwise there is nothing to connect the activity of which he is maintaining the profitableness with that whose profitableness the various speakers are considering. Moreover, Plato himself maintains this connexion when he makes Thrasymachus say that the just soul, i.e. the man whose parts work properly, will keep the ordinarily recognized commandments. And plainly Plato's own answer to the question which Thrasymachus answered by saying that justice is promoting the interest of the ruler is: 'Doing that in the service of the community for which our nature is best suited.'

What then is Plato's argument to show that the just man, i.e. the man who carries out his duty by serving the state, necessarily gains thereby? To answer this question we have to bear in mind that Plato's three parts of the soul are really certain capacities of desiring. This must be so, even though Plato introduces the rational part as reasoning, and afterwards speaks of it as exercising forethought on behalf of the whole soul. For his test for a difference of parts of the soul is the existence of a mental conflict, and the only things which can conflict are desires. Hence Plato must mean by the rational part of the soul the capacity for a desire of a special kind entitled to be called rational. In addition, the objects of this desiring part must be held to include the doing of what is just, i.e. serving the community. For he represents the just individual as one in whom the rational part is dominant, and so requires the doing of what is just, although the other parts prompt him to act otherwise. Plato must, therefore, be attributing to the just

[2] *Republic*, iv. 443 *b*.

man a desire to do his duty of serving the State, and maintaining it to be stronger in him than any other desire.

This being so, we can, of course, understand how Plato came to maintain that just action is in itself a good. For where we desire something, the thought that it is being or has been realized necessarily excites satisfaction, and if we desire to serve the State, either as serving the State, or as a duty, then serving the State, or (to speak accurately) the thought involved in doing it that we are serving the State, will necessarily itself excite satisfaction and so be a good to us, and we can distinguish its being thus in itself a good from the action's causing something which will be a good to us. But even so, strictly speaking what will be a good will not be serving the State, as Plato implies, but the thought that we are serving the State. And we can now see what he means when he says in effect that when we understand the nature of the just soul it is ludicrous even to ask whether the just man gains by his justice; viz. that just action will in itself excite in him a satisfaction so great as to outweigh any possible evils in the way of consequences. In fairness to Plato, however, two things should be noted. First, he seeks in Book IX to supplement the argument of Books I–IV by trying to show in detail that the pleasures obtained from satisfying the rational part of the soul are more permanent and less bound up with pain than those of the other parts. Second, at the end of the fourth Book he makes it clear that he does not go so far as to contend that any given man will *at once* gain in happiness by doing what is just, but is only contending that he will gain in the long run, first by a course of just action developing the just disposition (i.e. really the desire to do what is just), and then, though not before, by attaining a satisfaction, by doing what is just, which will outweigh all possible evils.

This being Plato's argument, what comments does it suggest? It has at least one outstanding merit. It does proceed on the only plan which has any hope of success, that of trying to make out that doing our duty is in itself a good so great as to outweigh any combination of resulting evils. For whatever be the kinds of action held to be our duty, since *ex hypothesi* they cannot be that of making ourselves happy (for if they were, there would be nothing to be proved), they must consist of acts causing things of another sort or sorts, and an act consisting of causing something of one kind cannot possibly be shown necessarily to cause something of another kind. Hence no consideration of the results of the acts held to be our duty can succeed in showing that we shall necessarily be the happier for doing them. And in this respect Plato's argument is only a special form of the endeavour to show that obedience to conscience is itself a reward sufficient even to outweigh any resulting evils.

Nevertheless, there is no denying that it is open to two fatal objections. The first is that even if for one whose desire to serve the state, or, alternatively, to do his duty, is at the maximum possible for any human being, the satisfaction excited by the thought that the object of this desire is realized would outweigh all possible resulting evils, yet any given individual may be incapable of having this desire developed to that extent, and so may not even in the long run become happier by doing what is just. Indeed, it is more plausible to say that the actions conducive to a given man's happiness will depend on his nature and that, e.g., if he is initially ambitious and little anxious to serve the state, he will gain most happiness by first developing and then gratifying his ambition rather than his desire to serve the state. And though Plato in Books VIII and IX does much to mitigate the force of this objection, what he says can only be a mitigation; and even Plato himself insists that those who, after contemplating the good, return to the cave to take their share of ruling and in doing so do what is just are making a sacrifice of happiness. And the second objection is that even for the man whose desire to do what is just is at the maximum possible for anyone, there must come a point at which, if the evils resulting from doing what is just continue to be piled up, they will outweigh the good to the man of knowing that he is doing what is just.

Here it may be noted that these objections are independent of Plato's view of what a man's duty consists in, viz. serving the state, so that if any other be substituted they still hold; and for that reason, in considering the success of Plato's argument, there is no need to consider whether he is right in thinking that what justice consists in is serving the state. The plain truth is, of course, that apart from theological reasons for thinking that the results of doing what we ought and doing what we ought not are specially adjusted by rewards and penalties, no general answer either way is possible to the question: 'Will doing our duty be for our happiness?' The only possible answer must be: 'It all depends; in some instances it may be and in others it may not.' . . .

In considering Plato's treatment of the connexion between duty and happiness, an underlying idea with which he approached the question has, for clearness' sake, been ignored. The idea lies in the background, and it may even escape notice. Yet it is undeniably there, and its presence explains the intensity of Plato's desire to prove that justice leads to happiness. Moreover, as the idea has not only been not infrequently shared by others, but may also affect either the questions asked about obligation or the answers given, its truth ought to be considered. The idea is one which concerns not how men ought to act but how they do act, and at first at least it strikes us as having little plausibility. It is that whenever we act deliberately, and not on an impulse, and so have a purpose, our final purpose, i.e. that the desire of which for its own sake leads us to do what we are doing and so forms our motive, is always the realization of our own good, i.e. of what will make us happy, or, more accurately, of our own happiness. The idea is one which Plato had formulated in the *Gorgias*,[3] where after contending that men do all that they do for the sake of the good (τὸ ἀγαθόν), i.e. as the context shows, of what is a good to themselves, he says of anyone who kills or exiles a man or despoils him of his wealth that he does it because he thinks it will be better for himself. In the *Republic* the idea first emerges in a rather disguised form at the beginning of Book II. There Glaucon is made to contend that men in fact only do what is just, i.e. their duty, ὡς ἀναγκαῖον, i.e. as an evil which has to be endured only to avoid a greater evil, and to urge in support that no one, like Gyges, able to do what is unjust with impunity would in fact do what is just. And that Plato himself here accepts this contention is shown by his representing Socrates, the mouthpiece of the truth, as having to show not that Glaucon's contention is mistaken, but that men in acting thus are mistaken in thinking just action the incurring the lesser of two evils. Later, however, in Book VI[4] the idea is explicitly stated, though in a way which may be misunderstood. There, in introducing the subject of the Idea of good, Socrates says that, while we are willing to put up with things which *seem* just and beautiful, it does not suffice us to obtain things which seem a good (τὰ δοκοῦντα ἀγαθά), but we seek things which are really a good (τὰ ὄντα ἀγαθά). And he goes on to speak of the good (τὸ ἀγαθόν) as that which every soul pursues and for the sake of which it does everything that it does, divining its existence, but perplexed about it and unable adequately to grasp its nature, and so misses such benefit as it might have got from other things. This statement, especially when taken in connexion with the earlier books, must be taken to mean that in all action what we are striving to bring into existence is—not what is good but—what is really good for us, or for our own good.

If we allow, as we must, that this interpretation is right, then we

[3] 468 *b*.
[4] 505 *d–e*.

can, of course, understand the intensity of Plato's desire to prove to us that we shall gain by doing our duty. For plainly he was passionately anxious for men to do what is just, and if he considered that men always seek their own good, he must have thought that men could only be persuaded to do what is just by being persuaded that it was the course of action by which they would gain. Also, we can then understand his contention that the ultimate question under consideration, for the sake of which he is considering whether justice is profitable, is: '*Should* or *ought* we to do what is just, i.e. our duty?' For this question will have the intelligible meaning of: 'Ought we to do our duty', in the non-moral sense of 'ought', i.e. is doing it necessary for the realization of our purpose in all action? And in view of what has been said, we may take it that this is the ultimate question to which Plato is addressing himself. We are, therefore, brought to the conclusion that the ultimate question which Plato is considering is: 'Should or ought we, in the non-moral sense, do our duty?' and that it is forced on him by his idea that men always pursue their own good. Further, *if* we share this idea, then for the reasons already given we shall have to conclude that the true answer is:

No general answer is possible; on some occasions it may be that we ought to do our duty, and on others it may not, but as we never know all the consequences to ourselves of an action, we never *know* whether we ought, in the non-moral sense, to do any particular action, whether a duty or not, though sometimes we may be able to have a fairly good opinion about it.

A FALLACY
IN PLATO'S
*REPUBLIC**

David Sachs

Recent writers on the *Republic* tend to refrain from detailed discussion of the argument about justice and happiness, the main argument of the work.[1] In the last decades there have been few assessments of Plato's conclusions about the relationship of justice and happiness, namely that just men are happier than any men who are unjust, and that the more unjust a man is, the more wretched he will be. Equally rare have been attempts to examine critically the argument by which Plato reached those conclusions.[2] In this paper I make such an attempt. My aim is to show that Plato's conclusions are irrelevant to what he sets out—and purports—to establish. The fallacy of irrelevance that, in my judgment, wrecks the *Republic's* main argument is due to the lack of connection between two conceptions of justice that Plato employs. I begin with an account of the two conceptions. While discussing them, I try to correct some errors and possible confusions about Plato's argument and his understanding of it. In particular, I try to show that Plato consistently viewed his defense of justice as one made solely in terms of justice's effects. I then examine the fallacy in detail. At the end, I briefly speculate about why Plato proceeded as he did.

* From *The Philosophical Review*, LXXII (1963), pp. 141–158. Reprinted by permission of the author and the editors of *The Philosophical Review*.

[1] "Justice," "injustice," etc. are notoriously unsatisfactory translations of many occurrences in Plato's dialogues of δικαιοσύνη, ἀδικία, and their relevant cognates. My use of the conventional translations does not, however, affect the claims of this paper. I am indebted to Mr. Gerald Barnes and Prof. Marshall Cohen for helpful discussion of some of the points I have tried to make.

[2] To my knowledge, the last detailed criticism of both Plato's procedure and conclusions is to be found in H. A. Pritchard's inaugural lecture, *Duty and Interest* (Oxford, 1928), and in the title essay of the same author's posthumously published collection, *Moral Obligation* (Oxford, 1949).

THE TWO CONCEPTIONS OF JUSTICE

Like other dialogues that have been called "aporetic" or "dialogues of refutation," *Republic* I ends with an avowal of ignorance by Socrates. Plato has him say that, not knowing what justice is, he can hardly know whether it is a virtue and whether its possessor is happy or not. An impression likely to be made by Socrates' last words in Book I is, as Richard Robinson remarked of the early dialogues as a whole, "that Socrates thinks that there is no truth whatever about x that can be known before we know what x is."[3] Robinson observes that though Socrates never actually says this, Socrates also never places any limits on the priority of answering questions of the form "What is x?" As a result, there is a general problem about the dialogues of refutation; do they include any assertions of doctrine by Plato?[4] Thus, in *Republic* I, Socrates makes various statements about justice; is his avowal of ignorance intended to question all of them? Certainly no doubt is cast upon one repeatedly implied claim, a claim taken for granted in the later books and presupposed by the over-all structure of the *Republic:* namely, that whether one should lead a just or unjust life is to be decided by determining which life is the happier.[5] It is, however, indispensable for evaluating the main argument of the *Republic* to realize that this claim cannot be understood in the same way throughout; it cannot, because of the two conceptions of justice in the *Republic.* I will call the first the vulgar conception of justice, the second the Platonic conception.

THE VULGAR CONCEPTION   Toward the end of *Republic* IV, immediately after the first exposition of the Platonic conception of justice, there is an important text for what I am terming the vulgar conception of justice. Socrates, speaking to Glaucon, says:

---

[3] Richard Robinson, *Plato's Earlier Dialectic* (2nd ed.; Oxford, 1953), p. 51.

[4] It is widely held that Socrates' professions of ignorance have to be discounted to some extent. For instance, Plato often—if not always—must have thought that the "absurdities" he had Socrates elicit really were absurdities. For an example in *Rep.* I, see 333e 1–2 *et supra.*

[5] See, e.g., 344e 1–3; 345a 2–7; 352d 5–6; 347e 2–4ff.; as these lines, together with the contexts in which they occur, show, the formulations in terms of an advantageous or profitable or better life are intended as equivalent to the formulation in terms of happiness. See also 392a–c; 420b–c; 427d; 472c–d; 484a–b; 544a; 545a–b; 578c; 580 *ad fin.*

We might . . . completely confirm . . . our own conviction . . . by applying . . . vulgar tests to it." "What are these?" "For example, if an answer were demanded to the question concerning that city and the man whose birth and breeding was in harmony with it, whether we believe that such a man, entrusted with a deposit of gold or silver, would withhold it and embezzle it, who do you suppose would think that he would be more likely so to act than men of a different kind?" "No one would." "And would not he be far removed from sacrilege and theft and betrayal of comrades in private life or of the state in public? . . . And, moreover, he would not be in any way faithless either in the keeping of his oaths or in other agreements. . . . Adultery, surely, and neglect of parents and of the due service of the gods would pertain to anyone rather than to such a man. . . . And is not the cause of this to be found in the fact that each of the principles within him does its own work in the mattter of ruling and being ruled?[6]

As Plato states them in this passage, the vulgar criteria for justice consist in the nonperformance of acts of certain kinds; and, of course, injustice, according to the vulgar conception, consists in performing such acts. The passage shows that Plato supposes that the just man—as he conceives him—is less likely than anyone else to perform those acts, to embezzle, thieve, betray, behave sacrilegiously, fail to keep oaths or agreements, commit adultery, neglect his parents or the service he owes to the gods. Plato thinks the conduct of his just man, far from being at variance with the vulgar conception of justice, will exemplify it.

The vulgar conception is shared at the start of the *Republic* by all of Socrates' interlocutors: Cephalus, Polemarchus, Thrasymachus, Glaucon, and Adeimantus. (This is not to say that the vulgar conception exhausts the notions of justice they hold, or that they all believe in behaving in accord with it.)

Thrasymachus, at 344a 3–5b 5, describes consummate (τελεω-τάτης) injustice and several kinds or "parts" (μέρη) of injustice; his list of kinds of injustice emphasizes gross types of immorality and evil-doing: temple-robbing, kidnaping, swindling, and so forth (see 348d 5–8). On Thrasymachus' view, to perpetrate such acts is to do injustice; not to commit them is essential to being just. Similarly, when Glaucon, for the sake of the argument, extols injustice, he finds it apt to relate the story of Gyges' ancestor, a man who seduced his king's wife, murdered the king, and usurped the kingdom; Glaucon

---

[6] 442d 10–443b 2; I have excerpted the passage from Shorey's translation in the Loeb Classical Library (Cambridge, Mass., Vol. I, 1937; Vol. II, 1942). Except where otherwise indicated, I use Shorey's translation.

then alleges that no one who enjoyed the impunity of Gyges' progenitor would "persevere in justice and endure to refrain his hands from the possessions of others and not touch them . . . [but would] take what he wished even from the market place and enter into houses and lie with whom he pleased, and slay and loose from bonds whomsoever he would" (360b 5–360c 2). Here, again, is a list of acts set forth as incompatible with justice and as constituting injustice. It should be stressed that the examples of unjust acts are presented by Socrates' interlocutors in such a way that it is plain they conceive the commission of any of them as injustice, and not committing any of them justice.[7]

THE PLATONIC CONCEPTION   Although the speeches of Glaucon and Adeimantus at the beginning of Book II give expression to the vulgar conception of justice, elements of the Platonic conception are also prominent in them. Commentators have often recognized that the speeches are vital for an understanding of how Plato conceives justice and for grasping what he tries to establish concerning it.

Glaucon, before his speech, asks Socrates if he really wishes to persuade them that it is in every way better to be just than unjust. The phrase "in every way" (παντὶ τρόπῳ, 357b 1) is then glossed by Glaucon's classification of goods and his and Socrates' discussion of it. The classification appears to be roughly the following: goods valued for their own sake, goods valued for their own sake and their effects, and goods valued only for their effects. The second type of goods is the one better in every way and Socrates says that, if a man is to be happy, he should thus regard justice; that is, value it both for its own sake and for its effects.

Plato's use of the expressions which I have conventionally rendered by the phrase "valued for their own sake" has perplexed readers about the main argument and aroused controversy.[8] The

----

[7] This statement of conditions for ἀδικία and δικαιοσύνη exhausts the notion of justice of Socrates' host, the scrupulous and fearful Cephalus; that Polemarchus shares much of the ordinary understanding of morality (and, unlike Thrasymachus, remains largely committed to it) is shown by the manner in which he reacts when Socrates reduces one of his positions to the absurd consequence that being just requires a "kind" of stealing (κλεπτική τις). See 334b 3–7. The few examples of injustice that Adeimantus gives are among those mentioned by Thrasymachus and Glaucon.

[8] E.g., αὐτὸ αὑτοῦ ἕνεκα ἀοπαζόμενοι (357b 6); αὐτό τε αὑτοῦ χάριν ἀγαπῶμεν (357c 1); αὐτὰ . . . ἑαυτῶν ἕνεκα . . . ἃν δεξαίμεθα ἔχειν (375c 8). For a compilation of the troubling expressions, see J. D. Mabbott, "Is Plato's Republic Utilitarian?," *Mind*, N.S. XLVI (1937), 469–470.

difficulty to which it has given rise is this: on the one hand, Socrates states to Glaucon that justice is to be valued for its own sake as well as for its effects, and Glaucon and Adeimantus stress in their speeches that they want Socrates to praise justice in itself (358d 1–2; 363a 1–2; cf. 367c 5–d 5); on the other hand, throughout the *Republic*, Socrates confines himself to an attempt to show that being just eventuates in happiness and pleasure for the just man; that is, he praises justice solely for what he alleges are its effects. Consequently, it has been charged that Plato, at the start of Book II, misconceived the task he thereafter tried to carry out; that he promised to prove that justice is good both for its own sake and for its effects, but addressed himself only to what he presumed were its effects.[9]

The expressions Plato uses are indeed likely to perplex contemporary readers, but an examination of the contexts in which they occur can help to remove the perplexity. When characterizing the first of the three types of goods, Glaucon says, "Are there not some which we should wish to have, not for their consequences, but just for their own sake, such as harmless pleasures and enjoyments that have no further result beyond the satisfaction of the moment?" The sentence just quoted is Cornford's very free translation of the problematic lines 357b 4–8; it has the merit, in comparison to other translations, of forcibly suggesting that αἱ ἡδοναί signifies activities or objects which produce pleasure, and not the pleasure produced.[10] The clause begin-

---

[9] A quarter of a century ago, M. B. Foster criticized Plato on this score (M. B. Foster, "A Mistake of Plato's in the Republic," *Mind*, N.S. XLVI [1937], 386–393). J. D. Mabbott replied, claiming that Plato does try to prove justice good for its own sake, or a good in itself (*op. cit.*). Foster, in answer to Mabbott, modified his criticism of Plato, saying that the vexing expressions made merely for a verbal ambiguity, "two different (and mutually inconsistent) ways of expressing what he [Plato] nevertheless conceived always as the same thing." According to Foster, Plato always meant to be claiming that justice is valuable because of its effects. Foster continued to maintain, in my belief rightly, that Plato did not try to prove justice a good in itself, or good for its own sake—in the sense which those qualifying phrases usually bear at present. See M. B. Foster, "A Mistake of Plato's in the Republic: A Rejoinder to Mr. Mabbott," *Mind*, N.S. XLVII (1938), 226–232. See n. 14 *infra*.

[10] F. M. Cornford (trans.), *The Republic of Plato* (New York, 1945), p. 42. Cornford's translation of τὸ χαίρειν (357b 7) as "enjoyments" is, at best, doubtful. (The occurrence of the phrase at 357b 7 poses, I admit, a difficulty—though hardly a decisive one—for my contentions in this section.) If, contrary to Cornford and following most translators, αἱ ἡδοναί at 357b 7 is taken to mean pleasure(s) rather than what produces it, the conclusion of Plato's sentence presents a considerable obstacle: since ταύτας in καὶ μηδὲν εἰς τὸν ἔπειτα χρόνον διὰ ταύτας γίγνεται ἄλλο ἢ χαίρειν ἔχοντα refers to αἱ ἡδοναί, it will have to be understood as pleasure which produces enjoyment, i.e. pleasure. Plato would then implausibly have to be understood as thinking that pleasure produces pleasure.

ning "that have no *further* result" should suggest that "for their own sake" is not being contrasted with "for (all and) any effects whatsoever" and that, instead, a distinction *among* effects is implicit. This is also suggested by the mention of enjoyment (χαίρειν ἔχοντα 357b 8), which one would naturally take to be an effect; indeed, if the sole effect of something is pleasure or enjoyment, it would appear to be an instance of the first type of goods in Glaucon's classification.[11]

When Socrates is asked where he places justice in the classification, he replies, "In the fairest class . . . amongst those which he who would be blessed, must love both for their own sake and their consequences."[12] Again, a present-day reader may wonder: how does Socrates conceive the relation of justice, which he places among the second type of goods, to blessedness or happiness? Socrates' remark is difficult, but Glaucon's comment on it is helpful: "That is not the opinion of most people. . . . They place it in the *troublesome* class of good things, which must be pursued for the sake of the reward and the high place in public opinion which they bring but which *in themselves are irksome* and to be avoided."[13] Glaucon's words are clear; according to the many, he is saying, justice in itself, since it is harsh or painful, should be avoided. The troublesomeness and harshness of it, then, are included under the heading "in itself." By analogy, the blessedness or happiness which Socrates thinks being just produces may be placed under the same heading. The need for discriminating the kind of effect intended by the phrases "in itself" and "for their own sake," from those intended by "effects" or "consequences" said *simpliciter*, is plain.

The distinction among effects is clarified by the repeated and virtually identical demands made of Socrates in Glaucon's and Adeimantus' speeches. Glaucon's request at 358b 4–7 is typical (see 366e 5–9; 367b 3–5; 367e 1–5; also 367a 1–8; 367c 5–d 5). He asks to be told the powers (δύναμεις) that justice and injustice, being present in the soul, exert *by themselves*—leaving aside the rewards and effects of both. From these passages it can be seen that Plato conceived of justice as good in itself, a good for its own sake, in terms of the effect which he supposed it exerted within the soul of its possessor. In the same way, he thought injustice an evil in itself. (The expressions literally translated by "for its own sake" and "in itself" might be paraphrased in a

---

11 For a surprising yet likely example, cf. 584b.

12 A. D. Lindsay (trans.), *The Republic of Plato* (New York, 1957), p. 44, 358a 1–3.

13 *Ibid.*, 358a 4–6; my italics.

less confusing way for present-day readers by the locutions "on its own" and "by itself.") For Plato, *no other* effects of justice and injustice were grounds for characterizing them as good or evil in themselves—and notably not those effects due to the knowledge or opinion others have of one's justice or injustice.

Glaucon's classification of goods, then, proves quite complex: first, items which by themselves (or on their own) are productive of good and of nothing else; second, those which by themselves are productive of good and, in conjunction with other things, have additional good effects; third, those which by themselves have bad effects but also have good ones which outweigh them.

Obviously, the classification is neither exhaustive nor neat, but if my account of the vexing phrases that occur in it and in Glaucon's and Adeimantus' speeches is correct, then Plato is not open to the charge of having promised to undertake what he never attempts.[14]

Plato's notion of the effects of the powers of justice and injustice in the souls of men is fundamental to the Platonic conception of justice (see 366e 5–6ff.; 367b 2–5). When Adeimantus complains that no one has adequately stated how justice and injustice, because of their powers, constitute respectively the greatest good and the greatest evil in the soul, he is anticipating theses Socrates will expound in Books IV, VIII, and IX. Adeimantus' speech is especially important because it repeatedly expresses Plato's aim of delineating the powers of justice and injustice as powers exerted solely by their existence or presence in the soul (see 366e 5–9). In this connection the word "power," though it correctly translates δύναμις, can prove misleading. For if it is conceived after the model of other uses of "power"—indeed on the model of other uses of δύναμις in Adeimantus' speech (e.g., 366c 2; 366e 4)—it will not be thought a power which *must* be exercised. What Adeimantus asks to be shown, however, is the good which justice inevitably works by its mere existence in the soul. Injustice, likewise, is to be proven an inescapable evil for the soul in which it is

---

[14] Even Foster's charge of verbal ambiguity (cf. n. 9 *supra*) should be dismissed. It imports into Glaucon's and Adeimantus' speeches a possibly anachronistic interpretation of "good for its own sake" and "good in itself," one in which those phrases mark a contrast with things that are good because of their effects, even when the good they produce is happiness or pleasure. As I have argued, Glaucon's and Socrates' remarks show that Plato did not intend this contrast. See 367c 5–d 2, where Adeimantus places justice among ἀγαθὰ γόνιμα τῇ αὐτῶν φύσει; cf. Adam's conjecture *ad loc.*, and Foster, in *Mind*, N.S. XLVI (1937), 392–393.

present. And these, of course, are the very demands Socrates attempts to meet in Books IV, VIII, and IX.

The most familiar evidence that Plato is intent on characterizing justice and injustice as things which cannot but work good and evil is, of course, contained in the famous similes of Book IV, where the just soul is compared to the healthy body, the unjust to diseased bodies, and the entire ἀρετή, or virtue, of the soul is called a kind of health and beauty and good condition, its contrary, κακία, being termed the soul's disease, ugliness, and enfeeblement (see 444c–e *et circa*).

If Socrates were to succeed in proving that justice by itself cannot but be good for the soul of its possessor, and injustice evil, he still would not be meeting Glaucon's and Adeimantus' challenge; for they ask him to show that justice is the greatest good of the soul, injustice its greatest evil. Further, showing this will not be sufficient unless Socrates thereby shows that the life of the man whose soul possesses justice is happier than the life of anyone whose soul is unjust. The latter is required of Socrates when Glaucon asks him to compare certain lives in terms of happiness. Glaucon envisages a just man's life "bare of everything but justice. . . . Though doing no injustice he must have the repute of the greatest injustice . . . let him on to his course unchangeable even unto death . . . the just man will have to endure the lash, the rack, chains, the branding-iron in his eyes, and finally, after every extremity of suffering, he will be [impaled]."[15] On the other hand, the unjust man pictured by Glaucon enjoys a position of "rule in the city, a wife from any family he chooses, and the giving of his children in marriage to whomsoever he pleases, dealings and partnerships with whom he will, and in all these transactions advantage and profit for himself," and so forth, including a not unreasonable expectation of divine favor.[16] Socrates has to prove that a just man whose condition is that described by Glaucon will still lead a happier life than anyone who is unjust if he is to show that, in terms of happiness, which is the Platonic criterion for the choice among lives,[17] one ought to choose the just life. Again, if Socrates is able to show that an unjust man who enjoys the existence depicted by Glaucon is more wretched than any just man, that will suffice for choosing to reject

15 Excerpted from 361c 3–362a 2; cf. the entire passage, 360e 1–362a 8.
16 Compare 613c 8–614a 3.
17 See the passages cited in n. 5 *supra*. Cf. also Foster, in *Mind* (1937), 387, and (1938), 229, 231–232; A. W. H. Adkins, *Merit and Responsibility, A Study in Greek Values* (Oxford, 1960), pp. 264, 283 ff., especially 290–291.

any unjust life. As Prichard remarked, "Plato certainly did not under-rate his task. Indeed, in reading his statement of it, we wonder how he ever came to think that he could execute it."

Some questions present themselves here. Assuming that the reader is acquainted with Plato's characterization of justice as a particular ordering of the parts of the soul, I will discuss these questions very briefly. Could Plato have thought it possible to lead a life which was neither just nor unjust? In Books VIII and IX he ranks kinds of souls according to degrees of injustice in them; might he have held that some souls lack both δικαιοσύνη and ἀδικία? On the Platonic conception of justice, the answer has to be no because, first, Plato is obliged to affirm, concerning numerous actions which may involve no one besides the agent, that they are done either justly or unjustly; for they, too, can alter the ordering, the polity or constitution, of the soul's parts. Secondly and decisively, even if one could avoid all actions that, on Plato's encompassing view, are just or unjust, the soul's parts would nevertheless be ordered one way or another; that is, either justice or injustice would be present (cf. 449a 1–5).

Another question, one often touched upon by H. W. B. Joseph in his *Essays in Ancient and Modern Philosophy*,[18] can be posed as follows. Few persons, if any, are perfectly just or consummately unjust; does Plato really try to maintain that all such intermediate lives are less happy than any perfectly just man's life would be? Since Socrates agrees that there are a variety of good things besides justice,[19] this question might be put by asking whether Plato really thinks that a life which includes an abundance of goods other than justice—but involves some injustice—must be less happy than, for example, the existence of Glaucon's beleaguered though just man. Anyone familiar with the *Republic* will know that this question has to be answered in the affirmative. Plato's consideration of the matter, it should be observed, is developed in terms of his own conception of justice. Thus in Book IV, Socrates states that there is one form of ἀρετή, or excellence, of the soul but limitless ones of κακία, or defect (cf. 445c 5–d 1; also 449a 1–5), four of which are worth special notice; they are the defects responsible for the timocratic, oligarchical, democratic, and tyrannical polities of the soul, the famous discussion of which occupies Books VIII and IX. There, while contending that the man whose soul possesses its ἀρετή is happier than any man whose soul lacks it, Plato tries

[18] Pp. 76, 80–81, 140–141, 153–154.
[19] See, however, *Rep.*, 491c–495a, 505a ff., 521a.

to determine which of the four forms of κακία produces the least un-happiness and which the greatest wretchedness. Clearly, what Plato attempts to establish—but again in terms of his own conception of justice—is that any intermediate life, any soul characterized by some degree of injustice, is inferior in point of happiness to the perfectly just, despite any other good things an intermediate life might include; and that the extent to which a soul is unjust is paralleled, *pari passu*, by the misery of the man whose soul it is (cf. 576b–e; 580a–c).

To summarize thus far: I began with the familiar observation that Plato held that the choice between the just life and an unjust life is to be decided by determining which is the happier. I then claimed that this position of Plato's is complicated by the presence in the *Republic* of two conceptions of justice, Socrates maintaining a distinctively Platonic one and Thrasymachus a vulgar one, while Glaucon and Adeimantus give expression to both. After stating the vulgar conception, I discussed some aspects of the Platonic one. In my discussion of the latter I tried to clarify what was meant when Socrates affirmed—and when Glaucon and Adeimantus insisted that he establish —that justice is good for its own sake or good in itself, and injustice evil in itself. Plato, I contended, characterized justice and injustice in these ways because he thought that on their own—or by themselves— they effect the soul's greatest good and greatest evil; this being due, Plato believed, to the powers which they inevitably exert upon the souls in which they are present. I further claimed that, on Plato's view, justice or injustice—one or the other but not both—must exist in every soul, and that the man in whose soul justice exists will be happier than a man whose soul includes any degree of injustice, happiness varying inversely with injustice.

In what follows, I argue that Plato failed to relate the two conceptions of justice adequately and that it is implausible to suppose that the omission, a complex one, can be repaired. Consequently, Plato's conclusions about happiness and justice—as he conceives the latter—prove irrelevant to the dispute between Socrates and Thrasymachus (and Glaucon and Adeimantus, in so far as they, too, are concerned with the happiness of vulgarly just and unjust men).

THE FALLACY

Toward the end of Book IV, Socrates formulates the Platonic conception of the just man: a man, each part of whose soul attends to its business or function, performing no tasks but its own. Further, Socrates says that if an action preserves or helps to produce the condition of the soul in which each of its parts does its own task, one ought to believe the action just and name it so, and believe an action unjust and name it so if it has a contrary effect (see 443e 4–444a 2). In accord with this, Socrates suggests that acting justly is to be understood as acting in a way which will produce the condition of justice in the soul, and that acting unjustly is to be understood as behavior which produces a contrary condition. Glaucon, I take it, is sounding a like note when he affirms that just acts are necessarily productive of justice, unjust ones of injustice (444c 1–3; 444c 10–d 2).

It will be recalled that Thrasymachus, in stating his position, mentioned among unjust acts temple-robbing, kidnaping, swindling, thieving, and so forth. This list, again, was enlarged by Glaucon's mention of sexual relations with whom one pleases, killing, freeing from bonds anyone one wishes, and so forth; that is, acts commonly judged immoral or criminal. The man of whom it was to be proven that his life will be happier than other lives is the man who does not commit such acts.

What Plato tries to establish, however, is that a man each of the parts of whose soul performs its own task, and who conducts himself throughout his days in such a way that this condition will remain unaltered, leads a happier life than any men whose souls are not thus ordered. Regardless of Plato's success or failure in this endeavor, for it to be at all relevant he has to prove that his conception of the just man precludes behavior commonly judged immoral or criminal; that is, he must prove that the conduct of his just man also conforms to the ordinary or vulgar canons of justice. Second, he has to prove that his conception of the just man applies to—is exemplified by—every man who is just according to the vulgar conception. For, short of this last, he will not have shown it impossible for men to conform to vulgar justice and still be less happy than men who do not. Plato had to meet both of these requirements if his conclusions about happiness and justice are to bear successfully against Thrasymachus' contentions and satisfy Glaucon's and Adeimantus' demands of Socrates. There are passages in the *Republic* which show that Plato thought there was no problem about the first requirement; there are, however, no passages which indicate that he was aware of the second. In any event, the fact is that he met neither requirement; nor is it plausible to suppose that he could have met either of them. Before I argue that this is the position as regards the main argument of the *Republic*, some objections which may be raised here should be faced.

For the purposes of this paper, which are the internal criticism and incidental clarification of the main argument of the *Republic*, I am not questioning—what have often been questioned—Plato's conclusions to the effect that men who are Platonically just are happier than men who are not, and that the farther a man's soul is from Platonic justice the more wretched he will be. My object is to show that these conclusions of Plato's are irrelevant to the dispute between Socrates and Thrasymachus and Thrasymachus' sometime advocates, Glaucon and Adeimantus. However, to press both of the requirements that I have stated may seem too stringent. It may be felt that, if Plato's conclusions are granted, he then need fulfill only the first requirement; that is, provide a demonstration that the Platonically just man cannot perpetrate vulgar injustice. For Plato's conclusions, together with such a demonstration, would have the consequence that the happiest men are among those who conform to vulgar justice; thereby, Thrasymachus' position would be refuted. But even granting Plato's conclusions, had he met the first requirement and not the second, he would have left open the possibility of Platonically unjust men who were vulgarly just and yet no happier, perhaps less so, than vulgarly unjust men. Alternatively, it may be thought that the satisfaction of the second requirement—namely, a demonstration that the vulgarly just man is Platonically just—would, together with Plato's conclusions, have sufficed. For it would then follow that no one was happier than vulgarly just individuals; and this, too, would refute Thrasymachus' position. It would, however, leave open the possibility of there being men who were Platonically just, and consequently as happy as anyone else, yet capable of vulgar injustices and crimes. Because of these considerations, both requirements had to be satisfied.

Both explicitly and by implication, Plato distinguished his special conception of justice from the ordinary understanding of morality.[20] Moreover, he repeatedly alleged connections between the two. In Book IV, after Socrates defines the virtues (441c–442d), he and Glaucon agree that the Platonically just man is least likely of all men to commit what would ordinarily be thought immoral acts; and in Book VI, Socrates attributes the vulgar moral virtues to men of a philosophical nature—to men, that is, whose souls are pre-eminently ordered by

[20] In addition to the passage cited in note 8 *supra*, see 517d–e and 538c–539d.

Platonic justice (484a–487a). Doubtless, then, Plato thought that men who were just according to his conception of justice would pass the tests of ordinary morality. But although Plato more than once has Socrates say things to this effect, he nowhere tries to prove it. Attempts to show that Platonic justice entails ordinary morality are strikingly missing from the *Republic;* Plato merely assumes that having the one involves having the other. The assumption, moreover, is implausible. On Plato's view, the fulfillment of the functions of the soul's parts constitutes wisdom or intelligence,[21] courage, and self-control; and if these obtain, justice, according to Plato, also obtains. Intelligence, courage, and self-control are, however, *prima facie* compatible with a variety of vulgar injustices and evil-doing. Neither as usually understood nor as Plato characterizes them are those virtues inconsistent with performing any of the acts Thrasymachus and Glaucon mention as examples of injustice. In this regard it is tempting to assert that the most that can be said on behalf of Plato's argument is that crimes and evils could not be done by a Platonically just man in a foolish, unintelligent, cowardly, or uncontrolled way.

In Books VIII and IX, where Plato sketches the degeneration of the polities of city and soul, the motives he uses to characterize the timocratic, oligarchical, and democratic types of soul are motives which, especially when strong, may lead to vulgar immorality and crime. But Plato, it should be noted, does not state or even suggest that it is inevitable for them to do so. By contrast, his account of the tyrannical soul, the opposite extreme from the Platonically just, is replete with the description of crimes that men who have tyrannical souls commit (573e–576a); their immorality and wickedness, aggravated if they become actual tyrants, is said to pertain necessarily to them (580a 1–7). However, the suggestion that men with souls of a timocratic or oligarchical or democratic kind are prone to perform immoral acts of course fails to satisfy the first requirement for Plato's conclusions to be relevant. And if it were granted that men whose souls are tyrannical are somehow necessarily evil-doers, this still would

---

[21] Because "wisdom," the orthodox translation of σοφία, is the name of something intimately connected with justice and morality as they are ordinarily understood, I suggest, as an alternative, "intelligence"; whatever Plato intended by his employment of σοφία toward the end of Book IV, one is not entitled to assume without argument that a man who possesses it will be ordinarily just or moral. There is some warrant for using "intelligence" because, in at least one relevant passage, Plato employs φρόνησις interchangeably with σοφία. See 433b 8 *et circa.*

not meet the requirement. That is, neither separately nor conjointly do the theses of Books VIII and IX about other types of soul exclude the possibility of men whose souls are Platonically just committing what would ordinarily be judged immoral acts. Any supposition to the effect that the theses of Books VIII and IX were meant by Plato to establish the claim that vulgarly unjust acts can be performed only by men whose souls lack Platonic justice is unconfirmed by the text of those books;[22] in any case, Books VIII and IX contain neither proof nor intimation of a proof for that further thesis.

The first requirement, then, is left unfulfilled. Plato merely has Socrates reiterate the implausible assumption a demonstration of which was needed. The second requirement, it will be recalled, is a proof that the vulgarly just man is Platonically just. While there are passages in the *Republic* which indicate that Plato thought there were no difficulties about the first requirement, the position is not even this favorable in regard to the second: he nowhere so much as assumes that men who are just according to the ordinary conception are also Platonically just. Indeed, there is no reason to suppose that this was his belief; but the omission of a claim to that effect within the framework of his argument cannot but seem surprising. Plato abundantly represents Thrasymachus, Glaucon, and Adeimantus as questioning the happiness of ordinarily just, moral men. It seems incontrovertible that when they ask to be shown how justice, because of its power, constitutes the greatest good of the soul, Glaucon and Adeimantus are taking for granted that the souls of vulgarly just men will enjoy the effects of justice. Nonetheless, an examination of Socrates' reply to Glaucon and Adeimantus (an examination, that is, of Book II, 367e to Book X, 612b) fails to uncover any claim whose import is that vulgar justice entails Platonic justice.

A remark I quoted earlier may seem capable of being drafted into Plato's service here. After Socrates and Glaucon agree that the Platonically just man is the least likely of all men to commit vulgar injustices, Socrates says, "And is not the cause of this to be found in the fact that each of the principles within him does its own work in the matter of ruling and being ruled?" (443b 1–2). Socrates is here stating that the cause of the Platonically just man's vulgar justice is

22 As I have stated, at other places in the *Republic* Plato makes unsupported claims tantamount to the assertion that if one's soul is Platonically just, one will be vulgarly just, and this of course implies that, if vulgar injustice is done, it is done by men whose souls lack Platonic justice.

precisely that he is Platonically just. Perhaps someone might be tempted, on the basis of the remark, to think that Plato was suggesting that Platonic justice is a necessary condition for vulgar justice. There is, however, no warrant for extending the remark in this way. Although Plato sometimes speaks of an item as the cause (αἰτία) of something where it seems that he thinks of it as a necessary condition of it (for example, when he speaks of the "forms" as causes at *Phaedo* 100c–d *et circa*), his uses of αἰτία are by no means always of this kind. Nor do I see any reasons for thinking he is so using it at 443b 1–2. A more likely construction of those lines would take them as equivalent to the claim that Platonic justice is sufficient to insure vulgar justice; that is, as equivalent to the implausible assumption, a proof of which is my first requirement.

Apart from the fact that Plato never states that being vulgarly just entails being Platonically just, one may wonder if such a claim is at all plausible. It does not seem to be; for instance, scrupulous, rule-bound men of the very type evoked by Plato's portrait of Cephalus at the beginning of the *Republic* provide examples of men who are vulgarly just but whose souls lack Platonic justice, and men with timocratic souls might provide additional Platonic counterexamples to the claim that vulgar justice entails Platonic justice.

My criticism of Plato's argument, it is worth observing, is unaffected by considerations of how he understood happiness (εὐδαιμονία) or blessedness (μακαριότης); and, again, my criticism is independent of the success or failure of his attempts to establish the happiness of *his* just man. Had Plato succeeded in showing that the happiest or most blessed of men are those who are just according to his conception of justice, and that the farther a man is from exemplifying Platonic justice the more unhappy he will be, Plato still would not have shown either that Platonic justice entails vulgar justice or the converse. That is, he would still have to relate his conclusions to the controversy which, plainly, they are intended to settle.

In conclusion, a speculation: it concerns one of the possible philosophical motives for Plato's conception of δικαιοσύνη. In the first interchanges of the *Republic*, the existence of exceptions to moral rules of conduct is emphasized. Plato has Socrates more than once assert—both of telling the truth and paying back or restoring what one owes—that it is sometimes just to do these things, sometimes unjust (ἐνίοτε μὲν δικαίως, ἐνίοτε δὲ ἀδίκως ποιεῖν, 331c 4–5; cf. 331c 1–332a 5 entire). Partly on this basis, partly because of similar passages in other dialogues, I believe it likely that Plato held that there are allowable exceptions to every moral rule, or virtually every moral rule, of conduct.[23] What is more, I believe that Plato was so impressed by what he took to be permissible exceptions to moral rules of conduct that his certainty of the existence of those exceptions, together with his certainty that no defining logos could have any exceptions, led him to—or confirmed him in—the view that rules of conduct do not constitute anything essential to morality or justice. This, I believe, was one of the principal motives for his characterization of δικαιοσύνη, a characterization not in terms of conduct and the relations of persons, but in terms of the relations of parts of the soul.

[23] Cf., e.g., the vexed passage, *Phaedo* 62a 1-7 *et circa; Symposium* 180e 4–181a 6; 183d 3-6. The remarks in Pausanias' speech in the *Symposium* are, of course, of dubious value as evidence for Plato's own views. For further discussion of the point and additional references, see G. Santas, *The Socratic Paradoxes and Virtue and Happiness in Plato's Earlier Dialogues* (unpublished Ph.D. dissertation, Cornell University, 1961), p. 68 *et passim.*

COMMUNISM
IN PLATO'S
*REPUBLIC**

Ernest Barker

When we turn from the subject of the new education to that of the new social order, we return once more to the organic view of the State. The communism which is peculiar to this new order is indeed still mediæval; it has its affinities with the communism of a monastery. But its theoretical basis is to be found in the philosophic conception of the State as an organism, and of justice as the duty of filling unselfishly and thoroughly an allotted place; and its practical basis lies in a reaction against the selfishness and ignorant inefficiency which marked contemporary Greek politics, as they appeared to Plato. It is a material and economic corollary of the spiritual method, by which Plato has already attempted to enforce his conception of the one, and to mark his reaction against the other. It receives perhaps more emphasis from Plato than these spiritual methods, because he is more conscious of its novelty and its need of justification. On the other hand, in spite of Aristotle's criticism, it cannot be doubted that it was primarily by spiritual means that Plato sought to regenerate man and society; and it must not be forgotten, that the material institutions of a communistic system are only meant to clear the ground and to remove the hindrances in the way of the operation of these spiritual means. This is implied in the fundamental conceptions of the *Republic*. The State is a product of mind, and to reform the State we must reform man's mind. Justice is nothing external, but a habit of mind; and true justice can only be realised when the mind acquires its true habit. Lastly, the realisation of the Idea of the Good is the ultimate condition of a proper State animated by true justice; and it is *education* which is necessary, if that realisation is to be attained. The spiritual motive is

* From *The Political Thought of Plato and Aristotle* by Ernest Barker (New York, 1906), pp. 137–162.

thus entirely and indubitably dominant. Herein lies a great and primary difference between Platonic communism and modern socialism. Without denying that socialism has its ultimate spiritual ends, we may assert without injustice, that it starts from materialistic conceptions to achieve a material result. It demands an equal division of material goods, for the sake of an equal diffusion of material happiness. Plato demands an equal abnegation of material goods, for the sake of that ideal happiness, which comes from true fulfillment of function. Where modern socialism is positive, Plato is negative: while in its tenets there is something of hedonism, in his there is only too much asceticism.

We have seen that Plato began the *Republic* with the idea of combating and destroying a false conception of the self as an isolated unit concerned with its own satisfaction. It is his aim to substitute a conception of the self as part of an order, and as finding its satisfaction in filling its place in that order. This conception, we saw, is expressed under the name of Justice, and it means that each man should do one special work truly and thoroughly, and that no man should selfishly and aggressively trespass on the province of his neighbour. Now communism is to Plato the necessary result of this conception of justice. *Two* of the three classes of his ideal State—the rulers and the soldiers—must, if they are to do their work truly, and to keep to it unselfishly, live under a *régime* of communism. They must not work with the part of their soul which is desire, if they are to devote themselves to the perfecting of their proper elements of spirit and reason; and they must therefore abnegate the economic side of life which is the outward expression of desire. If they threw themselves into that life, they would hamper the operation of the proper elements of their soul, both by letting them fall into disuse, and by indulging an element of the soul which is hostile to them. Accordingly, it appears that a communistic life, in the sense of a life divested of the economic motive, is necessarily connected with, and issues from, the supremacy in the State of the proper elements of mind, and particularly of the element of reason. Communism is postulated by the rule of the philosophic nature, in which reason is dominant. Without communism reason would either be dormant (while desire acted, and busied itself with acquisition) or, even when it acted, it would be troubled in its action by desire, which would tend to make it act for selfish ends. Not only is communism necessary to reason, but reason issues in communism. Reason means unselfishness: it means that the man whom it animates abnegates mere self-satisfaction as his aim, and throws himself into the welfare of a larger whole. And it means this because, in virtue of it, the philosophic temper realises the world as a scheme ordered towards the Idea of the Good, and recognises the State as a scheme within that scheme, and the individual, again, as in turn a part of that scheme. Through reason the philosophic ruler sees that he is an "organ" of the State, and that he must put away all the element of desire, since what is required of him as an organ of the State is pure reason.

Communism then *must* come, that reason may be perfect, and that by the perfect working of reason in its appointed place in the State, justice may be realised: while that it *will* come, reason is in itself the guarantee. But just because it is thus connected with reason, which is but one of the elements of the State, and an element represented by a far smaller body of citizens than any other element, communism cannot be a matter of the whole State, but only of the guardians and auxiliaries. Neither the communism in respect of goods, nor that in respect of wives, which are both advocated by Plato, touch the third or economic class. How indeed could a system which means the abnegation of desire touch the class which represents the element of desire? The third class has both property and families. Both, it is true, are under the strict supervision of the government. The government regulates trade and industry (less by law, than by its innate wisdom): true to the main principle of the *Republic*, it assigns to each member of the economic class his special work, in order that, each man practising his own craft, and no man interfering with that of another, there may be no dissensions; and it prevents producers from becoming either too rich or too poor, since both riches and poverty corrupt and destroy the State. But this is a policy of Protection, in its widest sense, and not of Communism: it is a policy, which admits an individualistic management of economics, but regulates it by considerations of the welfare of the State. . . . Unlike modern communism in his ideal aim, Plato is therefore unlike it also in his scope; and paradoxically enough, as it may appear to a modern mind, he invents a system of communism which has nothing at all to do with the economic structure of society—which leaves an individualistic system of production still standing, and does not touch a single producer. It must indeed appear a strange communism to any modern communist; for it is a communism in which, limited as are the divisors, the dividend is still less. The guardians to whom the system applies are distinguished from the rest of the State by sharing in a common poverty, like a body of Franciscan friars. Property they have none. Neither individually nor collectively do they own a single acre: the land and its products are in the hands of the third estate of farmers. They have no houses: they live in common barracks, which are always open and public. But on what, then, do they live? On a salary paid in kind by the farming classes according to a regular assessment, a salary paid year by year, and consisting of such necessaries as will suffice for the year. These necessaries are not divided among the guardians for private consumption: they are to be consumed at common tables. . . . It may be argued that fundamentally the same object characterises both Plato and the modern socialist. That object is, in a word, solidarity. The socialist aims at destroying the unchecked competition of individual with individual in the economic sphere, exactly as Plato sought to destroy, in the field of politics, the competition for power between one selfish unit and another; he aims at eliminating the gospel of the "economic man," as Plato sought to eliminate the preaching that might was right. Socialism attempts to realise the conception of a social whole, of which each man feels himself a member, and of a common interest, in securing which each man secures his own: Plato attempted to realize the same conception. Against both the same objection is and has been urged—"they destroy individuality": against neither is this objection properly valid, upon any true conception of the meaning of individuality.

But Plato's scheme embraces not only communism of property; it also contemplates communism of wives; and here, it may be said, a vital difference is obvious between modern aims and those of Plato. The difference may be doubted. Communism of wives in the sense in which it was advocated by Plato, may be understood most easily in its negative aspect, and as meaning the abolition of the family. . . . He wished the rulers of his ideal State to be troubled neither by distractions from their work, nor by temptations to self-interest. He had deprived them of property, since its care was a distraction, and the desire to gain it was a temptation. But his aim was only half-achieved with the abolition of property. The family postulates property for its maintenance: it is a distraction from the genuine work of a man's life; it is a temptation to throw oneself into self-seeking, which seems almost something noble, when it is disguised under the garb of a father's anxiety for the "future" of his children.

To Plato the "home," which is so precious to us, was anathema. "Every Englishman's house is his castle," we say. "Pull down the walls," Plato replies: "they shelter at best a restricted family feeling: they harbour at the worst avarice and ignorance. Pull down the walls, and let the free air of a common life blow over the place where they have been." For the ruler and the soldier there is but one home—and that is the State. Had they separate and individual homes, the result would be disunion among themselves, and separation from the subjects whom they should protect and govern. . . . Cumbered with material cares and the drudgery of serving tables, neither men nor women have time to be what they might be, or to take their place in the State. Occupied with necessities, they cannot heed counsels of perfection; struggling for mere life, they cannot think of the real life, which is the life of the spirit.

Plato approaches the reform of the household—with something of a desire for paradox, and a wish to tilt against convention—in the name of the emancipation of woman. Among the Greeks the life of woman approached more to the seclusion of Eastern manners, than to the freedom of the West; and the Greek girl received no other education than what the women's quarter of the house could afford. To Plato it seemed that this meant, not only that the development of woman was stunted, but also that the State lost the service of half of its members. While men had attempted to do all manner of works, and needed to be driven back upon one, women, he thought, had been allowed no single function (except that of child-bearing and child-rearing), and ought to be granted the right of discharging all for which they were fitted by Nature, not excluding the function of serving the State. In judging of their natural aptitudes Plato was guided . . . by an analogy. He had compared the guardians to watch-dogs in an earlier passage; and he now suggests that, after all, dogs of either sex can do the work of watching, with the one difference, that the female is somewhat weaker than the male. Against the application of the lesson which this analogy has to teach, it may be urged that there is a vital difference of nature and almost of kind between man and woman. Plato denies the difference: if woman differs from man in sexual function, she is in all the other functions of life a weaker man, possessed of the same capacities but not of the same strength. It is absurd, he argues, to make a distinction in one function the ground for a distinction in all; and he therefore assigns the same training and the same duties to men and to women alike—within the circle of the guardians. . . . For Plato is not a teacher of woman's rights so much as of woman's duties; and if he aims at emancipating women from the bondage of the household, it is only in order to subject them again to the service of the community at large. Yet such service is true freedom; in it woman stands by man's side as his yoke-fellow in the fulness of his life, and by it she attains the fulness of her own; nor must we, in speaking of Plato as the teacher of woman's duties, forget that he is, especially for a Greek, amazingly liberal in his attitude towards women.

But how is this scheme, which devotes woman to the service of the State, to be reconciled with the physical necessity of continuing the species? How can marriage, and the bearing and rearing of children, be dovetailed into a plan, which rejects the family, and (apparently) un-sexes the woman? Let us suppose for a moment that monogamy were still to be practised. The men-guardians, living in common and open barracks, have no place to which they can bring a wife: the women-guardians, living the same life and in the same way, can make no home for a husband. Under such conditions monogamy could only mean that the husband saw his wife occasionally (perhaps in his barracks, perhaps in hers), and that neither could attend to their children, ab-sorbed as both were by the State. But monogamy under such condi-tions, where the husband loses the society of his wife, and both lose the care of their children, loses its *raison d'être*. If therefore for any reason any other system of marriage should commend itself, it will be obviously preferable. A system of communism did commend itself to Plato, and a system of communism he accordingly adopts. He had two reasons for preferring that system. There was first of all a physical reason. The analogy of the animal world suggests that if you desire to have a good stud of horses, you must put a good sire to as many good dams, and a good dam to as many good sires, as you possibly can. To produce a good stock of citizens, the State must act on the same principle: it must supersede monogamy at will by communism under supervision. The Platonic State, which we have already seen charged with the duties of regulating the forms of literary composition and the methods of literary expression, must undertake to give its subjects in marriage. But it was perhaps the moral advantage of communism which appealed to Plato most. It will eliminate the motive of selfish-ness, and finally secure the solidarity of the State. Granted com-munism in the first generation—granted, too, that the State takes means to prevent the identification of children, by removing them from their mothers at birth—then, by the third or fourth generation, every mem-ber of the ruling and fighting classes will be generally related to every other, and no member will be (or at any rate no member will know that he is) particularly related to any other. Such a system of relation-ship will be to the advantage of the State, because it will make for its unity. Unity is secured when all the members of a body can say of the same thing, at the same time, and from the same point of view: "This loss is my loss: this gain is my gain". In other words, a body has attained solidarity when its members have so entirely identified themselves with the whole, that whatever happens to any part of the whole is felt by each member as happening to himself. Now such a perfect solidarity seemed to Plato to characterise a circle of relations. To make the State into a circle of relations will therefore tend to its unity, and so to its good. And thus the State is brought, according to Plato's desire, as near to the unity of the individual man as may be: if it has not become a single individual, it has at any rate become a single family. The political bond which unites citizen to citizen, has been strengthened by the tie of kinship and sentiment, which unites brother to brother: the warmth of domestic affection has reinforced the feeling of political fellowship. The new city, which Plato's imagination has compacted, is the home of its citizens, who know no other; it is their "fatherland," in deed as well as in word. The children who are born within it are all "children of the State," reared as it were in a *crèche*, and under the care of public nurses, until they are ripe for education.

By this new regulation of the relations of the sexes, Plato thus hopes to achieve many things—freedom for man and woman to develop their highest capacities, and to exercise them together as true comrades in their proper work; betterment of physique; complete and living solidarity. To the first of these results, and to the last, the new regulation of property would also, as we have seen, contribute. It is easy to agree with the aims which Plato proposes to himself, but it is somewhat difficult to accept the means; and here, as elsewhere, one may agree with Plato's principles, and yet reject their over-logical or over-driven application. Take for instance the principle, that a proper field should be given for the exercise of woman's capacities. The principle is perfectly true: the two means for its realisation seem both quixotic and impracticable. It is impossible that a woman should do everything that a man can do. The fact of her sex is not one isolated thing in a woman's nature, in which, and in which alone, she differs from man: it colours her whole being; it makes her able indeed to inspire noble enthusiasms, but not to direct a policy or to drill a regiment, as Plato would require his woman-ruler or woman-soldier to do. Again, it is impossible that men and women should come together merely for sexual intercourse, and instantly depart. They may meet primarily for that purpose, but ultimately, as Aristotle taught, they meet for a life's friendship, for the sake of a permanent interest in a common welfare; and in the "friendship" or permanent interest of true marriage lies one of the greatest influences towards a good life. Not only, however, does Plato make an unreal abstraction of the sexual motive, when he contemplates the regulation of that motive by the State for the sake of producing a good physique; he also makes of the individual a mere means, and that in respect of a side of life on which the individual most naturally claims to be an end to himself. In other words, he denies a fundamental right to personality, in a field where the sense of personality is most vivid, and where the whole man, body and soul, reason and feeling, "all thoughts, all passions, all delights, whatever feeds this mortal flame," cry for their satisfaction. It is indeed one of the most repulsive things in the *Republic* . . . that Plato should make his State a breeding establishment for the production of fine animals.

Under the whole scheme of communism, whether in property or in wives—underneath the whole attempt to abolish private possession and private life—there lies the assumption, that much can be done to abolish spiritual evils by the abolition of those material conditions in connection with which they are found. Spiritual medicines, it must always be remembered, are the first and primary cure in Plato's therapeutics; but a ruthless surgery of material things is also a necessary condition. Because material conditions are *concomitant* with spiritual evils, they seem to him largely their cause; and since to abolish the cause is to abolish the effect, he sets himself to a thorough reform of the material conditions of life. By compelling men to live under absolutely different conditions in the material and external organisation of their lives, he hoped to produce a totally different spirit and an utterly different attitude of mind. The gist of Aristotle's criticism of this conception is simple: spiritual medicines are all that one needs, or can use, for spiritual diseases. Educate a man to the truth, and by the truth that is in him he will connect the very same material conditions, which were before connected with evil, with everything that is good. Material conditions are concomitants, not causes; occasions, and not reasons; and it is idle to tinker with occasions. It is more than idle: it is corrupting and enfeebling. To free men from drudgery is not necessarily to make them live the free life of the spirit; . . . And is it not everywhere true, that to take away occasions of stumbling is to produce a weak-kneed godliness—that to shelter the soul from what may try its endurance is to produce at best a "fugitive" virtue? . . . Here again there is something mediæval in Plato—something of a horror of the world and its temptations. He does not, indeed, like a true mediævalist, fly from the world to the cloister: he would rather shatter and remould this sorry scheme of things nearer to his heart's desire. None the less there is a flight from the natural world in Plato; as there is in Aristotle something of the modern spirit, which would cheerfully accept whatever life can offer. Plato's attitude towards the world, like that of the mediæval mind, is based on pessimism: there is something evil in matter, with which the spirit would only contend in vain. . . .

It is obvious that Plato's attitude involves a certain element of reaction. Institutions, we have said, are a product of mind; yet he rejects many of the institutions of a civilised life. This may well seem inconsistent; and the question naturally occurs, why should the products of mind be rejected by a thinker, who believes that they *are* the products of mind, and can only reject them on the strength of the conceptions of his own intelligence? It is a question which a wise reformer must always ask himself; nor can it but dismay him to reflect that he is opposing his single mind to institutions, which have been created, maintained, and approved by the minds of many generations. Yet in one thought there is consolation. Were these institutions the products of *right* mind, of mind acting in view of a true end and by appropriate means? Error may become inveterate as well as truth; and it has often been seen that the suggestions of some powerful intelligence, when backed by the influence of a strong will and an attractive personality, may enter into the life of a whole people without real examination or discussion. The historian sees that they have entered and established themselves, and he readily believes in their sanctity, and accuses those who aim at their destruction of the want of a proper historical sense, and of forgetting that "the roots of the present lie deep in the past". None the less the philosopher has the right to inquire *how* they came, and to ask by *what* title they exist, and *what* element of mind they express; and if he is dissatisfied with the answer which he receives, he has every right to suggest, what *should* have come instead, what has a *real* title to exist, what element of mind *ought* to be expressed. But history deserves some respect, and Plato pays it little. He rejects the whole of its developments as so many mistakes, and substitutes in their place his own ideas of what ought to be. Aristotle's criticism is shrewd and dry. "We must not forget that we ought to attend to the length of past time and the witness of bygone years, wherein it would not have escaped men's notice, if these things had been right and proper." But, to tell the truth, Plato's ideas of "what ought to be" are not so much the undiscovered novelties of latter days, as the most primitive antiquities of the remote past. We spoke of an element of reaction: we might almost have spoken of atavism, and recurrence to the savage. In music, in medicine, in the reconstruction of society, this trait is prominent. The "luxurious" State is in his eyes suffering from a "fever": it needs a letting of blood, a purification. It must be brought back to simplicity, by which Plato means that the superfluous elements, which are not conformable to the spirit of justice, must be excised in order that the whole may attain to conformity. Back to simplicity it is accordingly brought, but the simplicity which is gained proves in the issue to be the simplicity of the primitive; and Plato falls into the ordinary error of finding the path of progress in the way of retrogression. . . . Again and again this tendency appears. Music is confined to the simple and direct expression of simple moods by means of simple instruments. . . . In Plato's theory of medicine the barbarian element is clear; and when one reads of the duty of the physician to leave those who are chronically sick to perish, one is reminded of the savage who helps the aged to die by exposing them to starvation. In the system of communism suggested by Plato it is impossible not to detect the savage once more. At the bottom of the communism of the *Republic* there is not only something of the "common tables" of Sparta, not only something of the Spartan customs of marriage, but also some knowledge of the supposed communism of wives among peoples, whose marriage customs there were no Greek ethnologists to explain scientifically as the result of exogamy, and some inkling of the communism of property, which appears to characterise the village community. Aristotle, we know, made a collection of "barbarian customs"; but logographers had already recorded these things when Plato wrote, and Sophists had already descanted on their ideal simplicity as the true *régime* of "Nature". Here as elsewhere Plato is the debtor, as well as the enemy, of the Sophists; although it must be remembered, that while the Sophist had found in primitive customs the means of dispensing with the State, which lost its *raison d'être* when it was no longer needed for the sanction of marriage and the guarantee of property, Plato used them for the stays and supports of an ideal State still more to be abhorred by every Sophist than the actual, because stronger and more disposed to interfere. Yet in the very conception of the unity of this ideal State there is a latent barbarism: it is a clan, knit together by the bond of blood. . . .

One final point of view remains to be raised with regard to Plato's communism. Does it, or does it not, destroy individuality? Is it compatible with the preservation of the rights of individuals? Does not Plato deny liberty in the name of fraternity (as he also sacrifices equality in the name of efficiency) when he institutes a philosophic despotism? It is certainly Plato's aim to destroy individuality of the false kind, to abolish individual "rights" as construed in the proposition "might is right," and to deny freedom in the sense of doing as one likes. But on the other hand it is as certainly his aim not only to guarantee but to develop individuality in the true sense of the word, and with it the rights and the freedom it requires. The individual is in reality, as we have seen, part of a scheme, a member of a whole. Such a conception of the individual is implied by a teleological conception of the world. If the world is one, and works towards one end, then the State is a part of the world, with an end subsidiary to its end, and the individual again is a part of the State, with an end subsidiary to the end of the State. Because the whole world is a co-ordinated whole, a single scheme and not a mass of units, the individual cannot stand by himself, but only in his place in the whole, and as playing his part in the scheme. Upon this conception, freedom will mean liberty to play that part freely: the rights of the individual will be those conditions which are necessary to playing that part, and which must be secured to the individual if he is to play it properly. Freedom in that sense, conditions of this kind, Plato certainly tries to secure. The whole system of communism is meant to set the individual "free" from everything which prevents him from taking his right place in the order of the State (and thereby in the order of the world): it is designed to secure those conditions—in other words, to guarantee those "rights"—which are necessary to the positive discharge of the right function, the function which helps the State to perform its function, and thereby the world to attain its end. But, it may be rejoined, this teleological conception cuts the individual short, and limits him to being and acting merely in the single aspect of a part. On the contrary, we may answer, far from cutting short, it broadens and expands. The self is the sum of its interests; and the individual is narrowest when he stands by himself, with no interests outside himself, and widest when he exists and acts as a part, identifying himself with the interests of the whole body of which he is a part. The wider the whole of which the individual can act as a part, the greater the sum of interests that he has, the greater is his individuality. The motto of life may be said to be "Live in as wide a fellowship as you may, and have fellowship in as many interests as you can".

Liberty then need not be sacrificed to gain fraternity: on the contrary, through fraternity man comes by the fullest and therefore freest use of his powers. No rights are destroyed when the individual is made part of a community: rights belong to the individual as a member of a community, and are the conditions of his action as a member, secured to him by the community. The teleological conception is "the foundation for all true theory of rights," because it involves this conception of the individual as a member of the community, acting for its end, and guaranteed the conditions of such action. That no sacrifice of the individual, or of liberty, or of rights, was involved by his philosophy Plato felt sure; and he argued the point under the rubric of happiness. He urged that his guardians were "happy," or enjoyed the sense of free and full play of their individuality which the Greek termed εὐδαιμονία, by acting in their appointed place in the State. "In a proper State," he tells us, "the individual will himself expand, and he will secure the common interest along with his own," because he has made it his own (497 A). Where, then, is the error of Plato's communism, in respect of its attitude to the individual? Granted that Plato has a true conception of the meaning of individuality, and a true conception of rights (as the conditions of the free activity of the individual considered as a member of society), is there not some flaw in his reasoning? He starts from right principles: may there not be here as elsewhere defects in their application? There would appear to be two. In the first place, while it is true that the self should grow and spread forth its branches, it is also true that it must have a root. A wide extension of interests may be desirable; but such an extension is of little avail, unless it has its basis in a strong personality and the conscious sense of an individual self (φιλαυτία). Unless we premise such a sense of self, that which identifies itself with a wide range of interests is— nothing; and the result is nothing. It is obvious that if the expansion of the self is to be a real thing, issuing in action and making for good, there must be a firm and steady basis for its support. It is the error of Plato that he forgot the basis, in contemplating the superstructure —that in aiming at the extension of the self, he forgot that it must have a previous intensity. Too often it is true that it is an ineffective, un-individual type of mind which identifies itself with a wide range of interests; and a strong sense of personality, though combined with a narrow range, will go further and do more for the world, than any watery altruism (ὑδαρὴς φιλία). The diffusion of the one type has to be reconciled with the concentration of the other; and we must first know ourselves as separate individuals, in order to transcend such knowledge, and to know ourselves as part of a wider order, and as serving a wider purpose. It is exactly this power of knowing ourselves as separate individuals which Plato really destroys, when he abolishes property; for property is a necessary basis of any conscious sense of an individual self.

This then is one flaw of Plato's communism, that by abolishing the basis of *any* sense of self, it takes away the possibility of the *true* sense of self which he inculcates. It does deny therefore to the individual a right—a necessary condition of his thinking and acting as a member of society and of expressing a social will; for it denies him that which is a necessary condition of his thinking and acting at all, and of expressing any will. The other flaw which may be traced in his reasoning is this, that he postulates of the individual, that he shall identify himself with no lower scheme nor order than that of the State. Such a postulate is impracticable and impossible. Every individual does and must identify himself with a lower scheme, and a narrower order—that of the family. It is true that the State is a fellowship (κοινωνία), "and each one of us part of it"; but it is also true that it is a fellowship of fellowships (κοινωνία κοινωνιῶν), and each one of us part of those—which is the great lesson that Aristotle teaches. It is true again that the State is a product of mind—that it is mind concrete in an external organisation: it is not true that the unity of the State is as the unity of a single mind, or that mind must be concrete in a single organisation, the "Republic one and indivisible".

The meaning and the bearing of the line of criticism here indicated may be realised more clearly, if we place ourselves at a point of view suggested by Plato himself, and regard the State as an organism—that is to say, as a whole of which the parts are organs for the attainment of a single end. Of such a whole the human body, whose members are all organs for the purpose of life, has generally been taken as a type. Now the application of the category of organism to the State is necessary and true. It is necessary, because it gives a true idea of the kind of unity which exists in the State: it is necessary, because it is an antidote to a false idea of the unity of the State, as legal in its essence, and contractual in its form. Modern political thought has borrowed from biology an organic conception of the State, which it has opposed to the legal conception of a contract entertained by thinkers like Hobbes and Locke, exactly as Plato drew from his teleology a similar conception, and opposed it to the "conventional" view of the Sophists. The emphasis which is now laid, as it was also laid by Plato, upon the organic character of the State, is just and salutary. A contractual conception degrades the State into a business partnership (*societas*), whose members are linked by a purely voluntary tie of self-interest. They have put as it were their money into a concern which they have called the State, because they thought that it would pay; and if they find that it fails to pay—as the Sophists argued that it failed to pay the "strong" man—they can and will withdraw from the concern. The organic view, on the contrary, substitutes a vital for the voluntary tie. It teaches that the unity of the State is not one made by hands, and by hands to be broken, but an inevitable outcome of human nature and human needs. It teaches that the State can no more be left by its members, than the body by its limbs, and that its dissolution is as much the death of its members, as it is of itself. While in this way it attaches the individual to the State, as the outcome of his nature and the essence of his being, in the same process it also links individual to individual, citizen to citizen. Members of one whole, the citizens are members one of another: as every limb seems to ache when one limb is pained, so the poverty and degradation of one class must impoverish the life of the rest; and the education and assistance of the weaker members is thus inculcated upon the stronger, as the very condition of their own welfare. The conception of a common weal and a vital union supersedes that of self-interest and a casual nexus.

The conception of a common weal is very present to Plato: the quality which he postulates in his guardians is a vivid sense of its existence. Union is very vital in his eyes: "there is no greater good than whatsoever binds the State together into one". But he may be accused of having pushed the organic conception too far, and of having attempted "to unify the State to excess" (λίαν ἑνοῦν). The conception is valuable when it is used negatively: it is dangerous in its positive application. A true organic theory of the State must recognise that, while the category of organism is one which partly covers the State, and, indeed, covers it better than any other category, it does not cover it entirely. In the first place, the State, if an organism, is one whose parts have a will of their own, and with that will the demand for its expression, and with that demand a right to private property, as a necessary subject upon and through which expression can take place. In the second place, the State is an organism whose parts are also members of other organisms. They are members for instance of the family, and the family is an organism whose end may be subsidiary but cannot be sacrificed to that of the State. Any organism which satisfies a vital necessity of human nature, like the family, must be indestructible, however detrimental to the organic unity of the State it may at first sight appear. But the zeal of the State had come upon Plato, and had come as a fire to consume whatever was not of the state. . . .

The line of interpretation which we have followed in dealing with the *Republic* now brings us to our final conclusion. On the one hand, the *Republic* is not a Utopia: it is a practical treatise on politics, written in reaction against contemporary political conditions, and, in its attempt at reconstruction, based upon contemporary facts. It is written to rebuke the intellectual and moral defects, defects of ignorance, defects of selfishness and corruption, which disfigured Athens and other Greek cities; it is written to commend to Athenian imitation the practices and institutions of Sparta. On the other hand the treatise, practical as it may be, has also a theoretical and ideal aim. It attempts to show what politics would be, if they were informed by the highest principle of justice, and what would be the manner of a State, in which the Idea of the Good had found its perfect expression. That politics ever should be after this fashion, that there should ever be a State according to this manner, Plato hardly expects; it must be an ideal to which men may approximate as closely as they can, but not a copy which must be imitated line for line. He well knows that the actual must recede far from the ideal: he also knows that the actual will not go far, unless it has a high ideal set before it . . . Yet there is some variation in his attitude, and while in one passage he speaks of the ideal State (in which justice and the Idea of the Good have been perfectly exemplified) as "laid up in the heavens for an ensample," elsewhere he thinks that what he has sketched is "no vision, but possible if difficult of accomplishment". And thus, it would appear, there is a certain oscillation between a practical attempt at construction, and the theoretical exhibition of a State based on ideal principles. It would be unjust, on the strength of this oscillation, to criticise Plato as though he had meant the whole of his scheme to be realised. But it is not unjust to criticise the theoretical exhibition of a State based on ideal principles, upon the ground that those principles are in their application pushed to an excess. And this is the line of criticism which we have attempted to take. Plato, as we have seen, had seized upon those principles, which are and always have been the fundamental principles of every State. He saw that the State is a product of mind: he saw that it is an organic unity. But, in the process of application, he pushed these principles to conclusions with which it is impossible to agree. If the State *is* a product of mind, it ought not therefore to be separated into three elements, nor should it be guided towards a purpose higher than it has grasped by the wisdom of one of these. If its unity *is* organic, that does not mean that the family must be abolished, or property destroyed. The tyranny of principles carries Plato too far. He speaks of a stage in the development of reason, when conscious of its powers it uses them as it were in play, for the purpose of contradicting everything, like a young puppy which fleshes its teeth by indiscriminate tearing and rending. It is a stage which one may perhaps detect in the

Sophists: they were the wandering "puppies" of dialectic, barking at conventions, and delighting in contradictions. But Plato had himself attained to a stage, when reason is still more masterful, and almost equally destructive. He had risen above contradiction to the eternal verity; and in the strength of his hold upon it he was too eager to enforce it upon the world for its salvation. He did not sufficiently recognise that the eternal verity had been working throughout history, if not consciously realised by man: he was too anxious to make its conscious realisation by the philosopher into a ground for attacking all its past works. Not only so, but with a stern logic he would have enforced truth to its utmost consequence. If art was moral, it should be made moral, and nothing but moral, in its form, its content, its every phase. This is not the way of truth or of success in practical affairs. In the realm of man's action there is and there must be an absence of utter logic. In the beginning of the *Ethics* Aristotle tells us that the subject with which Political Science deals (and in Political Science he includes the whole field of human action on its practical side), is one which does not admit of absolute exactitude. Political Science must start from principles which are only true "for the most part," and it can only arrive at similar conclusions. To Plato Political Science starts from absolute principles, and arrives at equally absolute conclusions. His principles have their truth: they have also their qualifications. Life ought to be directed by them: it can only be directed by them partially, even if we postulate with Plato an ideal ground for their operation.

THE SUN AND THE
IDEA OF GOOD
(*Republic VI*, 504e–509c)*

David Ross

A. Plato introduces [this] passage (504e–509c) by remarking that the definitions of the virtues (previously arrived at) in terms of a distinction of three elements in the soul were only a second best—'that in order to gain the clearest possible view of these qualities we should have to go round a longer way'. Justice and the other virtues can be completely known only in the light of 'something greater than themselves' (504 d 4). This 'greatest object of study' is 'the Idea of good, from which everything that is good and right receives its value for us' (505 a 2–4). The greatest possessions profit a man nothing unless what he possesses is good, and knowledge of anything profits him nothing unless he knows what is good. The superiority of good to everything else is further evidenced by the fact that while many people would choose to do and possess what seems just or noble, even if it is not so, no one is satisfied to possess what seems good. Every soul pursues what *is* good and for the sake of it does all that it does, divining that there is such a thing even though it cannot say what it is. No man will know adequately, or be a good guardian of, particular instances of justice or beauty, unless he knows in what respect they are good.

What Plato has so far vindicated for the good is supremacy in one particular respect, as an object of desire. Men may desire things that are not good, but only if they believe them to be good, and the deeper object of their desire is that which *is* good.

This does not exhaust, for Plato, the supremacy of goodness over all other Ideas; but to bring out the other aspects of its nature he adopts an indirect method. He will try to get light on the Idea of

---

* From *Plato's Theory of Ideas* by David Ross, 2nd edition (Oxford, 1953), pp. 39–44. Reprinted by permission of the Clarendon Press, Oxford.

good by studying first its offspring (506 e 3). He starts by equating particulars with what is seen, and Ideas with what is known (507 b 9). Here sight stands for sense in general, for a particular sound is a particular none the less because it is not seen but heard. But Plato goes on to point out a respect in which sight is distinguished from the other senses—that in order that sight may occur there must be not only a coloured object and an eye capable of seeing, but also light playing on the object, and, best of all, the light of the sun. Just as the eye sees most clearly when its object is bathed in sunlight, the mind apprehends most clearly when it views its object in the light of the Idea of good. It is this that 'gives to objects of knowledge their truth, and to him who knows them his power of knowing' (508 e 1–3). And as neither light nor sight is the sun, neither truth nor knowledge is the good. The good is something even more to be honoured than they.

After saying what he does of the Idea of good as the source of knowledge and of knowability, the principle of explanation of the world of Ideas, Plato proceeds to exhibit it in a new light, as the source of that world's being. As the sun 'gives to visible objects not only the power of being seen, but also their generation and growth and nourishment', so 'you may say of the objects of knowledge that not only their being known comes from the good, but their existence and being also come from it'. But while the life-giving power of the sun is quite different from its illuminative function, the function of the Idea of good as source of the being of the other Ideas is really the same as its function as source of our understanding of them; for we shall be right in explaining the existence of the other Ideas by reference to the Idea of good, only if it is actually the ground of their being.

If we are to attempt even dimly to understand Plato's meaning, we must first realize that the functions assigned to the Idea of good are assigned to it in relation not to the sensible world, but to the world of Ideas; it plays the part in relation to them that the sun plays in relation to sensible things. In saying what he does of it he is not stating, directly at any rate, a teleological view of the world of nature. What he is saying is that the Ideas themselves exist and are known by virtue of their relation to the Idea of good. What can be the meaning of such a view of the world of universals? It is reasonable to offer a teleological explanation of some or all of the facts of nature, if we believe either in a benevolent Governor of the universe, or in a nisus in natural objects towards the good. But a teleological explanation of the world of Ideas is in a different position. Ideas are not changeable things, plastic to the will of a Governor; they are standards to which a Governor of the universe must conform. Nor on the other hand can we conceive of the Ideas as having a nisus towards good (though a passage in the *Sophistes* has often been misinterpreted as ascribing 'movement' to them); things may have a nisus, but universals cannot. It is, therefore, difficult to see what Plato can have meant when he says that the Idea of good accounts for the existence and the knowability of the world of Ideas. Nor are we helped by what he says later about the 'unhypothetical first principle', which is undoubtedly to be connected with the Idea of good; the only difference is that while the phrase 'the Idea of good' points to a universal, the other phrase points rather to a proposition, presumably one in which the Idea of good is a term.

We may consider first the relation of the Idea of good to other *ethical* Ideas. What Plato wishes to convey is presumably that the essence of each of the virtues consists in some relation to the good—that it is by virtue of this relation that they exist, and in the light of it that their nature can be understood. There are hints of this view in other dialogues. In the *Laches* Plato had said that knowledge of good and evil is the essence of the several virtues (199 d 4–e 1). In the *Hippias Major* he had said that we pursue φρόνησις and all other fine qualities because their product and offspring, the good, is worthy of pursuit (297 b 2–7). In the *Phaedrus* he defines temperance as the being guided by the desire of the best (237 d 6–e 3). We must suppose that on such lines as these he believed the essence of all the virtues to consist in some definite relation to the Idea of good.

That this is part of Plato's meaning is shown by the introductory passage already referred to. What he has in mind is the possibility of defining the virtues by reference not to parts of the soul, but to the precise relation of each to the *summum bonum* of human life. We may suppose that, as he thought of wisdom as being essentially knowledge of the good, he thought of courage, temperance, and justice as being essentially pursuit of the good in spite of the solicitations of fear, of self-indulgence, and of covetousness. The Ideas of the virtues will then owe their being and their intelligibility to the Idea of the good, and for them the Idea of the good will be 'beyond existence in dignity and power'.

But Plato assigns to the Idea of good, in other words to goodness or excellence, a much wider significance than the ethical significance we have considered. He describes it as 'giving to the objects of knowledge'—to all of them—'their truth, and to him who knows them his power of knowing'. Here it becomes harder to follow his meaning, and any interpretation must be conjectural.

For Plato ἀρετή, the quality which answers to the adjective 'good', is not limited to human goodness; everything in the world has its own characteristic excellence. In the *Gorgias* he speaks of the goodness of the body, and of the goodness 'of each thing, whether it be an implement or a body or a soul or an animal'. This thought is specially prominent in the *Republic* itself. He speaks there of the goodness of dogs and horses, of eyes, ears, and all other things, of the body, of each implement and animal. In other words he ascribes to everything in the sensible world an ideal excellence which is to it as the end of human life is to men. In these passages there is no direct reference to the Ideas. But in one passage this notion of an ideal excellence is linked with the Ideas. In the *Phaedo* he says that the not quite equal things with which the senses acquaint us aim at or aspire to 'equality itself', the Idea of equality. In this vein of thought—to which also belongs Plato's frequent description of the Idea as a pattern and of the particular as a copy—all the Ideas are thought of as types of excellence, as species (we may perhaps say) of the great generic Idea of excellence itself, and as intelligible only in the light of that Idea.

Many interpreters of Plato have said that in his system God and the Idea of good are identical; but this view cannot be maintained. It would be truer to say two things: First, that while any Idea, and therefore the Idea of good, is for Plato always a universal, a nature, wherever he speaks of God he means a being having a nature, and in particular not goodness but a supremely good being. This is already clear in the *Phaedo*, where, in Socrates' account of his mental history, reason, i.e. the divine reason, is clearly distinguished from the good to which it looks in its government of the world. Again in the early part of the *Republic*, where Plato maintains that the citizens of the ideal state must be taught that God is good (379 b 1), he clearly means that they are to be taught, not that goodness is good, but that the Governor of the universe is good.

But secondly, in the metaphysical section of the *Republic* very little use is made of the conception of God. It is not until we come to the *Sophistes* that we find Plato maintaining that complete reality belongs not only to unchanging Ideas but also to that which lives and thinks, not until we come to the *Timaeus* that we find the functions of the Demiourgos and his relation to the Ideas clearly set forth, and not until we come to the *Laws* that we find the Ideas to have receded from view, and God to hold the central place in Plato's thought. Yet it is worth noting that even in the present passage there is a foreshadowing of the *Timaeus*, when Plato speaks of the artificer (δημιουργός) of the senses (507 c 6).

The view that the Idea of good is, in Plato's thought, identical with God is to a large extent based on a passage in the *Sophistes* in which Plato has often been thought to ascribe 'movement, life, soul, and reason' to the Ideas. But it will be seen later that this is a complete misunderstanding (though a very natural one) of that passage, which concludes with the assertion that reality includes both that which does not change (the Ideas) and that which does (souls divine and human).

In what he says of the Idea of good Plato comes nearer, perhaps, than he does anywhere else to the expression of a transcendental philosophy, and it was largely on this passage that the Neoplatonists based their interpretation of his doctrine.

THE FOUR STAGES
OF
INTELLIGENCE*

Richard Lewis Nettleship

Having described in a general way the position and function of the good in knowledge, Plato goes on to distinguish more in detail the stages of development through which the human mind passes or might pass from ignorance to knowledge, from a point at which the objective world is, so to say, perfectly dark and unintelligible, to a point at which it is perfectly luminous. He represents to us by a very obvious symbol an ascending scale of mental states and a corresponding scale of objects of thought. Imagine a vertical straight line, and divide it into four parts. The line must be conceived of as beginning in total darkness at one end, and passing up to perfect light at the other. It is a continuous line, though it is divided into sections. Plato, in choosing this symbol, may have wished to express the continuity of the process which it represents. At any rate we have to remember that there is no sudden break between the visible and the intelligible world, which the two main sections of the line stand for.

The scale which the four sections of the line represent is a scale of luminousness. It is an attempt to represent the stages through which the human mind must go if it would arrive at a perfect knowledge of the world; and, again, an attempt to represent the different and successive aspects that the world presents to the human mind as it advances in knowledge. When we speak of the objects of the mind's thought in its different stages, we should divest ourselves of the notion that they represent four different classes of real objects; they only represent four different views of the world, or different aspects of the same objects. For what we call the same object has very different aspects to different people; for example, the scientific botanist and the person who knows

* From *Lectures on the Republic of Plato* by Richard Lewis Nettleship (New York, 1901), pp. 238–258. Taken from notes of lectures given 1885–88.

no botany may see the same flower as far as the eyes go, but they understand it in totally different ways; to the former it is the image of all botanical laws. Plato is anxious throughout to emphasize the difference between these views of things. They differ in degree of superficiality and profundity as well as of obscurity and luminousness. This means, we may regard progress in knowledge as a progress from the most superficial to the most penetrating view of things. Hence the relation between each higher and each lower stage is expressed by Plato as the relation between seeing an image or shadow and seeing the thing imaged or shadowed. This metaphor bears a great part in his theory of knowledge. It means that there is a great deal more in what the mind perceives at each stage than in what it perceives in the stage below. There is more in the actual solid object than there is in a mere reflexion or picture of it; and when science comes and says that these solid objects, which we call the real things in the world, are not the ultimate truth, that it is the principles which they embody which are really worth knowing, that not some particular plant or animal, but the permanent and uniform nature which appears in all such things, is the object of real knowledge, then science, though it seems to be leaving the real world behind, tells us more than the ordinary view of things tells us.

Through these different stages all human minds which develop their powers of understanding fully must more or less pass; the most gifted as well as the least begins by what Plato calls seeing things as images; different minds advance to different distances in different stages, and the same mind advances to different stages with different parts of itself. Plato's ideal for education is that, recognizing this law of mental development, it should provide for different minds by giving them, according to the stage they are in, appropriate objects of thought, and should lead them gradually, according to their capacity, and as easily as may be, to the truest view of things of which they are capable. Want of education in this sense means that minds which ought to have advanced further remain in a lower stage, and mistake the comparatively superficial view of truth they get there for the whole truth.

The four stages of mental development are called (beginning with the lowest) εἰκασία, πίστις, διάνοια, and νόησις (later called ἐπιστήμη). The two former are stages of what has previously been described as δόξα; the two latter are stages of what has been called γνῶσις or ἐπιστήμη and is later on called νόησις (a term which in this passage is limited to the higher of them).

(1) The most superficial view of the world, that which conveys least knowledge of it, is called by Plato εἰκασία. The word has a double meaning; it has its regular meaning of conjecture, and an etymological meaning of which Plato avails himself, the perception of images, that state of mind whose objects are of the nature of mere images (εἰκόνες). There is a connexion between the two meanings; when we talk of a conjecture we imply that it is an uncertain belief, and we imply also that it arises from a consideration of the appearance or surface of the thing in question. Plato has availed himself of both meanings of the word, so as to express a certain character or property of the object of mental apprehension and a certain state of mind in the subject; the mental state is one of very little certitude, its objects are of the nature of 'images,' shadows and reflexions.

Why does he describe this lowest group of objects as shadows or reflexions? Shadows, images, and dreams, are the most obvious types of unreality, and the contrast between them and realities is very striking to early thinkers, as it is to a mind which is just beginning to think. In what respect does a shadow differ from the real thing? It resembles it merely in the outline, and that is often very vague and inexact; the rest of the real thing, its solidity, its constitution, even its colour, vanishes in the shadow. In what respect does a reflexion differ from the real thing? A reflexion reproduces more of the real object than a shadow does; its outline is very fairly defined and exact; the colour of the object is retained to a certain extent; but a reflexion is still only in two dimensions. Any state of mind of which the object stands to some other object as a shadow or reflexion does to the real thing, is εἰκασία.

This at once opens an enormous field; but what particular states of mind had Plato in view? We may find an example of his meaning in the Allegory of the Cave, the prisoners in which see only shadows of images (ἀγάλματα). An instance of an image, in the language of that allegory, would be the conception of justice as embodied, perhaps, in Athenian law, which according to Plato would be a very imperfect embodiment. A step further from reality, a shadow of that image, would be the misrepresentation of the Athenian law by a special pleader. Suppose a man believed that justice really was this misrepresentation, his state of mind would be εἰκασία; justice would come to him through a doubly distorting medium, first through the medium of Athenian legislation, and further through the words of the lawyer.

We may take another example from Book X, where Plato works out this idea in his attack on the imitative arts. The effect of arts like painting is due to the fact that the artist puts before us not the actual thing, but its image (εἴδωλον) or its appearance at a certain distance. He puts things before us not 'as they are' but 'as they appear' (the word εἰκασία is not used, but it is the same idea). He is so far like a man who goes about holding up a mirror before things. If any one then were so far taken in by the perspective and colouring as to think the picture before him the actual thing, he would be in a state of εἰκασία. The moment a man knows that a shadow is only a shadow, or a picture only a picture, he is no longer in a state of εἰκασία in that particular respect. But, though the arts do not produce illusion of that simple kind, Plato attacks them in Book X, entirely on the ground that they are constantly used to produce and stimulate a multitude of illusory ideas of another kind. He takes painting as the most obvious instance of imitative art, but he applies the principle which he makes it illustrate to words. Poetry and rhetoric are the great sources of the kind of illusion he has in mind. The poet gives us an image of his experience; but, if we think we know all about a thing after reading about it, we are just as much deluded as if we took a picture for the reality. When then Plato talks of 'images,' he is not thinking specially of pictures or statues, what he is primarily thinking of is images produced by words. Sensitiveness to the force of words is a marked feature of Plato; and he seems to have felt intensely the power of evil they may have when used by a skilful sophist, as if his own great mastery over them had made him realize the possible perversion of such skill. He looks upon language as the power of putting images between men's minds and the facts. He felt this about rhetoric still more than about poetry, the two being closely associated in his mind, and both being arts of using language which exercised a great power over the Greeks.

But we must not suppose that Plato regarded the power of language as only a bad thing, and incapable of good. In Book III we have the metaphor of images used in a good sense; and we learn that it is one of the functions of art (including both poetry and the plastic arts) to put before us true images of self-command, courage, generosity &c., and to train the mind to recognize them. The scholar, he says, who knows his letters must be able to recognize them just as well in their reflexions in water or in a mirror, and so the μουσικός will recognize the types of beauty and the reflexions of virtue in art. Thus μουσική is conceived in this passage as the education of εἰκασία, a training of the soul to read the reproductions of reality in art aright; it is intended to develop rightly that side of the soul on which it is appealed to by images, a condition of mind which is predominant in children and undeveloped races, and in many men throughout their whole lives. In

Book X, on the other hand, where Plato denounces imitative art and exposes its dangers, all that he says is dominated by the idea that the artist gives us *only* the external appearance of things. His general view of art may be thus expressed: the right function of art is to put before the soul images of what is intrinsically great or beautiful and so to help the soul to recognize what is great or beautiful in actual life; when art makes people mistake what is only appearance for what is more than appearance, it is performing its wrong function.

We are all in a state of εἰκασία about many things, and to get a general idea of the sort of views that Plato had in mind when he spoke of shadows and reflexions which are taken for realities we must think how many views there are which circulate in society and form a large part of what we call our knowledge, but which when we examine them are seen to be distorted, imperfect representations of fact, coming to us often through the *media* of several other men's minds, and the *media* of our own fancies and prejudices.

The literal translation of εἰκασία is 'imagination.' But it would be very misleading to translate the one word by the other; for, while εἰκασία expresses the superficial side of what we call imagination, it does not express the deeper side. Imagination in English has two senses. In one sense it really does answer to Plato's conception of seeing images. When we say that something is a mere imagination, or that a man is the slave of his own imagination, we do mean to describe a very superficial view of things. But when we say that a poet is a man of great imagination we mean almost the exact opposite. We mean that the appearance of things suggests to him all kinds of deep truth which to the ordinary person it does not suggest at all. The great poet, while it is true that he regards things on their sensuous side, is great because he reads through what his senses show him, and arrives by imagination at truths not different in kind from those which another might arrive at by what we call thinking. Plato seems much more impressed by the possible misuse of imaginative work than by its possible use, though he himself is a standing example of what the union of thought and imagination can do. And it is an undoubted fact that we are apt to live habitually in an unreal world in which we take the image for the reality, instead of reading the reality by the image.

Plato's conception of the mental condition of the great body of men is put before us in the Allegory of the Cave; their state is for the most part such that all that occupies their minds is of the nature of shadows; it is, further, such that they firmly believe these shadows to be real and the only reality. And in this lies their illusion, for so long as a man realizes that the shadows are shadows there is no illusion. Their state is also one of great uncertainty. Among the prisoners in the allegory those who are honoured and rewarded most are those who are quickest at learning to remember the order in which the shadows pass, and who are thus best able to prophesy what will pass next. This is meant to illustrate how uncertain or conjectural their judgments necessarily are. In proportion as our knowledge is not first-hand, not derived from actual contact with things, we ought to regard our beliefs as uncertain.

(2) Thus εἰκασία is conjecture, and the next stage, πίστις, is so called because it contrasts with εἰκασία in regard to certitude. Πίστις is a feeling of certainty. When people have themselves come in contact with things, they feel far more certain about them than if they had only come into connexion with them through others, and πίστις is the state of mind in which we know what we call the actual tangible things of life; these are not the sole reality by any means, yet we feel about them a good deal of certainty.

We must remember that both εἰκασία and πίστις are subdivisions of 'opinion' (δόξα), so that what has been said of it is true of them. To the state of mind called opinion truth and reality exist under the form of a number of separate and apparently independent objects, each with a character and position of its own, whether these objects are real or reflected. Whether, for instance, one's knowledge of justice is derived from books or from what we are told, or derived from personal experience, it is equally true that, so long as we are in the state of 'opinion,' the only answer we could give to the question What is justice, would be to point to some particular acts or laws or institutions. Still we feel a difference when we come out of the region in which we can only know things at second hand, or can only imagine them, into that in which we have to do with them ourselves. It is the transition from uncertainty to a sort of certainty.[1]

Further, just as there is a good state of εἰκασία and also a bad state, a state which contains some truth and a state which contains none, so it is with all opinion. It is important to remember this, for in Book III 'right opinion' is the sum of virtue, the virtue of the Guardian; so that it is surprising to us when, in Book V, Plato begins to speak of

---

[1] The state of 'right opinion' described in Books III and IV, with its attendant virtue of courage, i. e. tenacity, is a state of πίστις. It is a state of mind which is continually being tested by action, as contrasted with a previous state of mind in which the soul was not in contact with real life.

opinion in a tone of contempt. Now εἰκασία is only described as a state of mind which we have to get out of, when it is regarded as one which we are satisfied with and accept as final; the harm of the shadow or reflexion arises only when one takes it for something else; illusion is the misinterpretation of appearance, but the appearance which is the occasion of illusion is capable also of being rightly interpreted. And so with opinion generally; it is only so far as one believes the object of opinion to be ultimate truth that it is a thing to get rid of. 'Right opinion,' in which true principles are embodied however imperfectly, is a state of mind which is quite laudable, and beyond which we cannot get as regards the great bulk of our experience. What is unsatisfactory in this state of mind is that it is bound up with certain particular objects, and is liable to be shaken when we discover that these objects are not so fixed and permanent in their character as we thought, but depend on their surroundings for their properties. Then the mind is set to ask, If what I have known as justice, or beauty, or weight, changes in this extraordinary way, when seen in different relations, and is in such a continual state of fluctuation, what can justice, or beauty, or weight be?

It is this feeling or perception that the objects of δόξα are self-contradictory which sets the mind to ask for other forms of truth. The sense of difficulty and embarrassment arising when what we are accustomed to believe in fails drives us to look for something else. We are impelled to search for what Plato calls 'forms,' principles or laws which make these various things what they are, or for the unity which underlies this changing and manifold world.

(3) Plato calls the stage of mental development in which he describes us as beginning to do this, διάνοια. The word itself gives no clear idea of the thing meant; it was to the Greeks what the word 'intellect' is to us. Like intellect, it has no very fixed meaning, and describes no one state of mind, but it was a word obviously applicable to the state of mind of which the scientific man is the best instance. Plato's illustrations of διάνοια are taken from the only sciences of his time; and, though there are differences, there is a great substantial similarity between the things he says of it, and modern ideas of what we should call the scientific habit of mind.

Plato gives us two characteristics of this state, without showing us the connexion between them: (*a*) It deals with sensible things, but it employs them as symbols of something which is not sensible; (*b*) it reasons from 'hypotheses.' Arithmetic and geometry are the most obvious types of διάνοια in both these respects.

(*a*) The arithmetician and the geometrician, while they use visible forms, are not actually thinking of them. The geometrician is thinking about the triangle or the circle as such; he uses the circle which he draws as a symbol of this; and though, without such symbols, the study of mathematics would be impossible, the circle which he draws remains a mere symbol. Visible images such as he uses are just the objects of opinion—separate, independent, sensible things, each with a position and character of its own. The objects of which these 'real things' are symbols to him are what Plato calls forms, such as the 'form of the triangle' or 'the triangle itself,' for these two expressions are used indifferently.

What Plato here says of mathematics applies to all science whatever. All science treats the actual objects of experience as symbols. It is always looking for laws, and the sensible things around us become to it symbols of them, or, in other words, are looked upon only as the expression of principles; the botanist or zoologist has to speak of particular animals or plants, but it does not matter to him what particular animal or plant of the same species he takes. We express the same fact by saying that science is abstract. The man of science necessarily and consciously leaves out of account a great deal in the objects he contemplates, and fixes his attention on certain points in them. It is a matter of indifference to the geometrician, in investigating the relations between the sides and angles of a triangle, how big, or of what colour, or of what material the particular triangle is; it may be of great interest to some one else, but not to him; yet all these things go to make up the 'visible triangle.' In using this phrase and contrasting the 'visible triangle' with an 'intelligible triangle,' which is the object of the geometrician's study, we are speaking as if there were two triangles, and may easily be led to think of the 'intelligible triangle' as if it were another triangle which is a faint image of the sensible one. From this difficulty of language arises the greater part of the difficulty of Plato's idealism. We must, therefore, be clear what we mean when we speak of the intelligible triangle; the use of the phrase does not imply that there are two different classes of triangles, the intelligible and the sensible; it means simply that there is in the sensible triangle a property distinguishable from all its other properties, which makes it a triangle. The sensible triangle is the 'intelligible triangle' *plus* certain properties other than triangularity. These other properties the geometrician leaves out of account, or, in Plato's language, regards as merely symbolic. The phrase, which is familiar to us, that science abstracts, expresses just what Plato means when he says that science treats particular objects as merely symbolic, symbolic of something which they as a whole are not. All science does this.

We may put this in a different way so as to illustrate its bearing upon education. The study of the sciences compels us to think; it compels us, as Plato says, to let go our senses and trust to our intellects. In Book VII he insists upon this in the case of all the sciences he mentions; we have in each to set aside our senses and their associations, and to look at things with our minds; that is we have to set aside all but that particular law or principle which is our object of interest for the time being. That is why science seems at first to upset all our ordinary associations and to be less real than our ordinary experience.

(*b*) Plato tells us further that διάνοια reasons from 'hypotheses.' We mean by a hypothesis a theory temporarily assumed to be true, which we are prepared to abandon if the facts do not agree with it; a hypothetical view would mean a provisional view, awaiting confirmation or disproof. But the use of the word ὑπόθεσις in Plato and Aristotle is different from this. Plato meant by a hypothesis a truth which is assumed to be ultimate or primary when it really depends upon some higher truth; not that it is untrue or could ever be proved false, but that it is treated for the present as self-conditioned. The point of contact between Plato's use of the word and ours is that, in both, a 'hypothesis' is regarded as conditional or dependent upon something; but Plato's hypotheses are by no means provisional theories, they are the truths at the basis of all the sciences. Arithmetic and geometry rest upon certain assumptions or hypotheses. The ultimate assumption of arithmetic is number, with its primary properties of odd and even. The arithmetician does not expect to have to give an account of this; if any one denies the existence of number, the possibility of his studying arithmetic is destroyed; but, granted number as a starting-point (ἀρχή), the arithmetician reasons from it connectedly and consistently, and discovers from it any particular arithmetical truth he wants. So with the geometrician; what he takes as his starting-point is the existence of geometrical space with a few of its most elementary properties. If, when he brings a truth back to his postulates, axioms and definitions, you deny them, he can only say it is impossible to argue with you; it is not his business as a geometrician to prove them. In the same way the physicist starts with the conceptions of matter and motion, the biologist with life, the economist with wealth, the moralist with morality. These, with a few of their most elementary forms and attributes, are the hypotheses of the sciences concerned with them, and each science has similarly its own hypotheses.

By calling such conceptions hypotheses, in the sense that they depend for their validity on some other truths, what does Plato mean? Not that they are untrue, for he speaks of them as a form of 'being.' They are hypotheses because, if we saw things wholly and as they are, we should see that being is one whole (a κόσμος), and that, as it is one whole, the various forms or kinds of it must be connected; whereas the arithmetician and the geometrician treat their respective forms of being as if they were perfectly independent; that is, they assume them without giving an account of them. The truths they start from await the confirmation (βεβαίωσις) of being shown to be elements in an interconnected whole. It is thus an imperfection of διάνοια that its 'starting-points' are hypothetical, that they are not seen in their true or full connexions; for the ideal of science is perfect connexion and perfect explanation. And these are the same thing. As long as you can ask Why? the ideal of knowledge is not satisfied. To ask Why? is the same as to ask What is this dependent on? Perfect knowledge would imply seeing everything in its dependence on an unconditional principle (ἀνυπόθετος ἀρχή). The human mind, though it never reaches such a principle, is always demanding it, and, so long as it falls short of it, cannot attain the ideal of knowledge. This points the way to the description of the final stage of intelligence, νόησις or ἐπιστήμη.

(4) This, as Plato describes it, is a pure ideal; to realize it is not within the scope of the human mind. But it expresses his idea of what we should aim at and what knowledge tends towards. It involves, he tells us, first, a state of perfect *intelligence* with no element of sense in it. It involves, secondly, the absence of hypothesis; the various principles of the specific sciences would be seen not as hypotheses but as they really are, all naturally following from the fact that the world is a world of reason, each being a step to the one above it, and so leading ultimately to the unconditional principle on which they all depend.

(*a*) The statement that in perfect intelligence there is no element of sense perception (nothing αἰσθητόν) is difficult to understand. Probably we may explain it in the following way. Take, by way of example, any object regarded by a geometrician, and used by him as a 'symbol,' say a triangle. We have seen that the real object which he thinks about is not that particular triangle, but the triangle as such. There remains therefore in the sensible object a great deal which is no object for the geometrician, but falls outside his intellectual vision. It is to him of the utmost importance that he should ignore it, that he should not confuse what makes the triangle a triangle with a certain size or colour. Otherwise, having seen a triangle an inch high, when he came to see another a foot high, he would suppose the properties of the two as triangles were different. In such a simple case no educated person would make such a mistake, but in more complicated things we are always making it, and it is because he thinks mathematics train men not to do this that Plato insists on their educational value. . . . Now the other properties of the triangular object, which are ignored by the geometrician, may of course themselves be made the subjects of scientific investigation. The student of optics may investigate its colour, some one else its chemical composition, and so forth. And so with more complex objects; every single property of any object has what Plato calls a form; as there is a triangle as such, or a form of triangularity, so there is colour as such, or a form of colour. Every particular object is the meeting-point of innumerable laws of nature, or, as Plato says, in every particular object many forms communicate. Suppose then that different men of science had set themselves to work to exhaust all the properties of an object, and that all these properties came to be understood as well as the triangularity of a triangle is understood by the geometrician, we should regard the object as the centre in which a number of laws of nature, or what Plato would call forms, converged; and, if an object ever were thoroughly understood, that would mean that it was resolved into forms or laws. The fact would have become a very different fact, a fact which, so to say, had a great deal more in it, though none the less a fact; the object as it is to an ignorant person would have disappeared. Therefore in perfect knowledge there would be no element of sense; not that anything which our senses tell us would be lost sight of, but that every sensible property of the object would be seen as the manifestation of some intelligible form; so that there would be no symbolic or irrelevant element in it, and it would have become perfectly intelligible. . . . It would not be a confused collection of properties which seem to be constantly changing and constantly contradicting themselves, but a meeting-point of various permanent and unchanging forms or principles. That is to say, it would take its place in an order or system of 'forms'; it would be seen in all the relations and affinities which it has. This is an ideal; but we do know that everything has relations and affinities with everything else in the world, and the only way in which we can represent to ourselves perfect intelligence is by supposing a mind to which all the properties of everything, all its relations and affinities with other things, are thus perfectly understood. This remains a true statement of the ideal of our intelligence, though of the great bulk of things our experience must be always to a large extent 'sensible.'

(*b*) In perfect intelligence there would moreover be no hypothesis. To describe how the world would present itself to a perfect intelligence, Plato uses a figure; it would present itself as a sort of scale or series of forms of existence, each connected with the one above it and the one below it, and the whole unified by one unconditioned principle, the good. The good is that on which they all depend, and that which, to use another figure of Plato's, is reflected in them all; or, again, the position and function of each in the world are determined by the supreme purpose of the world, the good. To a perfect intelligence it would be possible to pass up and down this scale of forms without any break, so that from any one point in the world it could traverse the whole. In proportion as we do understand one fragment of truth, one subject, we find it possible to start anywhere and to get anywhere in it and in the subjects most closely connected with it; and a very fair test of how far one understands a thing is the extent to which one can develop any given point in it. Such a state of mind in its perfection would be νόησις or νοῦν ἔχειν in the fullest sense of the words.

And here Plato introduces a new term. The power or faculty, he tells us, by which such a state of intelligence could be brought about is that of dialectic (τὸ διαλέγεσθαι, elsewhere διαλεκτική). This term he eventually uses to describe knowledge as it would be if perfect; and the passage in which he then introduces it throws light on the passage before us. Speaking of the application of the various specific sciences in his system of education, he says that if the study of them is to be made profitable to the end in view we must try to see their relations with one another. This is a principle to be borne in mind throughout the more advanced part of the education in science which he proposes; the points of contact between the sciences must be perpetually brought out. The test, we are told later, of whether a man has the dialectical nature is whether he is συνοπτικός, which means whether he has the power of seeing together at one view the relationships (οἰκειότητες) between the various specific branches of knowledge. Now this brings out strongly, what is hinted at in the passage before us, that progress in knowledge is progress in the perception of the unity of knowledge. A man who has a gift for perceiving this is a natural dialectician, and dialectic in the fullest sense is simply what knowledge would be if this possibility of seeing the affinities and communion between the different branches of knowledge (not, of course, only the particular sciences to which Plato refers, but all branches of knowledge) were realized. In this use of the word dialectic is equivalent to perfect knowledge.

PLATO
ON
POETRY*

Eric A. Havelock

It sometimes happens in the history of the written word that an important work of literature acquires a title which does not accurately reflect the contents. A part of the work has become identified with the whole, or the meaning of a label has shifted in translation. But if the label has a popular and recognisable ring, it can come to exercise a kind of thought control over those who take the book in their hands. They form an expectation which accords with the title but is belied by much of the substance of what the author has to say. They cling to a preconception of his intentions, insensibly allowing their minds to mould the content of what they read into the required shape.

These remarks apply with full force to that treatise of Plato's styled the *Republic*. Were it not for the title, it might be read for what it is, rather than as an essay in utopian political theory. It is a fact that only about a third of the work concerns itself with statecraft as such. The text deals at length and often with a great variety of matters which bear on the human condition, but these are matters which would certainly have no place in a modern treatise on politics.

Nowhere does this become more evident to the reader than when he takes up the tenth and last book. An author possessing Plato's skill in composition is not likely to blunt the edge of what he is saying by allowing his thoughts to stray away from it at the end. Yet this terminal portion of the *Republic* opens with an examination of the nature not of politics but of poetry. Placing the poet in the same company with the painter, it argues that the artist produces a version of experience which is twice removed from reality; his work is at best frivolous and at worst dangerous both to science and to morality; the

---

* From *Preface to Plato* by Eric A. Havelock (Cambridge, 1963), pp. 3–15, 20–31. Reprinted by permission of the Harvard University Press.

116

major Greek poets from Homer to Euripides must be excluded from the educational system of Greece. And this extraordinary thesis is pursued with passion. The whole assault occupies the first half of the book. It is clear at once that a title like the *Republic* cannot prepare us for the appearance in this place of such a frontal attack upon the core of Greek literature. If the argument conforms to a plan, and if the assault, coming where it does, constitutes an essential part of that plan, then the purpose of the whole treatise cannot be understood within the limits of what we call political theory.

PLATO'S ARGUMENT

To the over-all structure of the work we shall return a little later. Let us for a moment consider further the tone and temper of Plato's attack. He opens by characterising the effect of poetry as 'a crippling of the mind'. It is a kind of disease, for which one has to acquire an antidote. The antidote must consist of a knowledge 'of what things really are'. In short, poetry is a species of mental poison, and is the enemy of truth. This is surely a shocker to the sensibilities of any modern reader and his incredulity is not lessened by the peroration with which, a good many pages later, Plato winds up his argument: 'Crucial indeed is the struggle, more crucial than we think—the choice that makes us good or bad—to keep faithful to righteousness and virtue in the face of temptation, be it of fame or money or power, or of poetry—yes, even of poetry.' If he thus exhorts us to fight the good fight against poetry, like a Greek Saint Paul warring against the powers of darkness, we can conclude either that he has lost all sense of proportion, or that his target cannot be poetry in our sense, but something more fundamental in the Greek experience, and more powerful.

There has been natural reluctance to take what he says at face value. Plato's admirers, normally devoted to his lightest word, when they reach a context like the present start looking around for an escape hatch, and they find one which they think he has provided for them. Just before this peroration, has he not said that poetry may offer a defence of herself if she can? Has he not confessed to her overpowering charms? Does he not admit reluctance to expel her, and does this not mean that in effect he recants? He does indeed so confess, but to think that his confession amounts to a recantation profoundly mistakes his intention. Indeed, the terms in which he makes the concession to poetry, to plead her case if she chooses, are themselves damning. For he treats her in effect as a kind of prostitute, or as a Delilah who may seduce Plato's Samson if he lets her, and so rob him of his strength. She can charm and coax and wheedle and enthral, but these are precisely the powers that are so fatal. If we listen, we dare to do so only as we counter her spell with one of our own. We must repeat over and over to ourselves the line of reasoning we have previously followed. We must keep on our guard: 'We have our city of the soul to protect against her.'

The mood of this passage uncovers the heart of the difficulty. Plato's target seems to be precisely the poetic experience as such. It is an experience we would characterise as aesthetic. To him it is a kind of psychic poison. You must always have your antidote ready. He seems to want to destroy poetry as poetry, to exclude her as a vehicle of communication. He is not just attacking bad poetry or extravagant poetry. This is made even clearer during the course of the argument he builds against her. Thus the poet, he says, contrives to colour his statement by the use of words and phrases and to embellish it by exploiting the resources of meter, rhythm and harmony. These are like cosmetics applied as an outward appearance which conceal the poverty of statement behind them. Just as the graphic artist employs illusionism to deceive us, so the acoustic effects employed by the poet confuse our intelligence. That is, Plato attacks the very form and substance of the poetised statement, its images, its rhythm, its choice of poetic language. Nor is he any less hostile to the range of experience which the poet thus makes available to us. He can admittedly represent a thousand situations and portray a thousand emotions. This variety is just the trouble. By his portrayal he can unlock a corresponding fund of sympathetic response in us and evoke a wide range of our emotions. All of which is dangerous, none of it acceptable. In short, Plato's target in the poet is precisely those qualities we applaud in him; his range, his catholicity, his command of the human emotional register, his intensity and sincerity, and his power to say things that only he can say and reveal things in ourselves that only he can reveal. Yet to Plato all this is a kind of disease, and we have to ask why.

His objections are taken in the context of the standards he is setting for education. But this does not help us one bit to solve what seems at least a paradox in his thought, and perhaps, if judged by our values, an absurdity. For him, poetry as an educational discipline poses a moral danger, and also an intellectual one. It confuses a man's values and renders him characterless and it robs him of any insight into the truth. Its aesthetic qualities are mere frivolities and provide unworthy examples for our imitation. Thus argues the philosopher. But we surely, in estimating the possible role of poetry in education, would turn these judgments upside down. Poetry can be morally uplifting and inspire us to the ideal; it can enlarge our moral sympathies; and it is aesthetically truthful in the sense that it often penetrates to a reality as to a mystery which is denied to prosaic intellects. It could do none of these things in our eyes without the language and the images and the rhythm which are its peculiar possession, and the more of this kind of language you can put into a humane educational system the better.

Small wonder, as we have said, that Plato's interpreters have been reluctant to take him at face value. The temptation in fact to do otherwise is overwhelming. Was not the master a great poet himself, commanding a style which if it chose could abandon abstract argument in order to appeal to all the resources of the imagination either by vivid portraiture or by symbolic myth? Could a writer of such sensitive prose have really been indifferent, nay hostile, to the rhythmic arrangement and the verbal imagery which are the secrets of the poetic style? No, he must have been ironic or temporarily petulant. He cannot, surely, have meant what he said. The attack on poetry can and must be explained away, cut down to size, rendered innocuous enough to fit our conception of what Platonism stands for.

So runs subconsciously the argument, and like all such it reflects the modern prejudice which finds it necessary from time to time to save Plato from the consequences of what he may be saying in order to fit his philosophy into a world agreeable to modern taste. This may be called the method of reduction—a type of interpretation that can be applied also to certain facets of his politics, psychology and ethics—and it consists in pruning his tall trees till they are fit to be transplanted into a trim garden of our own making.

The pruning process has been applied quite liberally to that section of the *Republic* which we are looking at now. Several types of instrument have been used for the purpose, and applied to different parts of the argument. On the over-all issue, Plato is accommodated to modern taste by arguing that the programme of the *Republic* is utopian and that the exclusion of poetry applies only to an ideal condition not realisable in the recognisable future or in earthly societies. One might reply that even in that case why should the Muse of all people be selected for exclusion from Utopia? But in fact this kind of evasion of Plato's argument depends as we have said upon the assumption that the *Republic* (so-called) is all about politics. Is that not the label on the bottle? Yes, it is, but we must recognise that the contents of the bottle when tasted in this instance report a strong flavour of educational but not of political theory. The reforms which are proposed are considered to be urgent in the present and are not utopian. Poetry is not charged with a political offence but an intellectual one, and accordingly the constitution which has to be protected against her influence is twice defined as 'the polity within the soul'.

The critics have sought another instrument of evasion by supposing that the more extreme parts of Plato's polemic are directed against a passing fashion in literary criticism which had been fostered by the Sophists. They, it is argued, had sought to use the poets artificially as a source of instruction in all useful subjects, and had pushed these claims to absurdity. This explanation will not work. Plato to be sure speaks of the 'champions' of poetry but without identifying them as professionals. They seem rather to be the more vocal representatives of common opinion. He also speaks of these claims as though Homer himself were pushing them; that is, as though public opinion shared this exaggerated opinion of Homer. As for the Sophists, it is not usually remarked, as it ought to be, that Plato's argument here counts them not as his enemies but as his allies in the educational battle he is waging against the poets. This may not conform to the critics' usual preconception of where to place the Sophists in relation to Plato, but for the moment at least Plato has placed them in a context which prohibits the belief that in attacking poetry he is attacking their view of poetry.

Defensive criticism has yet another weapon in its armoury: this is to argue that Plato's target, at least in part of what he says, is not to be identified with poetry as such but is to be confined to drama and even to certain forms of the drama which followed a current fashion of extreme realism. The text however simply cannot stand dismemberment in this fashion, as though Plato at one point focused on Homer, Hesiod and drama, and at another point on drama alone. It is true that tragedy is in the forefront of his mind, simply because, we suggest, it is contemporary. But the striking thing is his constant refusal to draw a formal distinction between epic and tragedy as different genres, or between Homer and Hesiod on the one hand (for Hesiod is also mentioned) and the tragic poets on the other. At one point he even uses language which suggests that 'tragedy', that is drama, is a term by which to define all poetry, applying equally to 'epic and iambic'. It makes no difference, he seems to imply, whether we mean Homer or Aeschylus. He defines the subject matter of the target he is attacking as: 'Human action, whether this action be autonomous, or the result of external compulsion, and also including what men think or feel about their actions; that is, how they interpret their effect in terms of weal or woe to themselves, and their corresponding joys and sorrows.' This definition applies as vividly to the *Iliad* as to any stage play. Indeed, Plato goes on to illustrate what he means by citing the poet's description of a father's grief at the loss of his son. This plainly is a reminiscence of an instance cited earlier in the *Republic*, where Plato is thinking of Priam's collapse at the loss of Hector.

Scholars would not have been tempted to confine Plato's target in these contexts to the drama were it not for the fact that the philosopher does seem to be occupied to a rather extraordinary extent with the emotional reaction of an audience to a public performance. The reason for this preoccupation will be unfolded in a later chapter. It does indeed supply one of the clues to the whole puzzle of what Plato is talking about. In our modern experience the only artistic situation which can provoke such public response as he describes would be the performance of a stage play. So we are tempted to conclude that Plato has his eye exclusively on the stage, forgetting that in Greek practise epic recital equally constituted a performance, and that the rhapsodist apparently exploited a relationship to his audience analogous to that of an actor.

These attempts to lessen the impact of Plato's assault do so by trying to disperse it over a variety of targets. They are well-meaning, but they misconceive the whole spirit and tenor of the argument. It forms a unity; it is launched, as we shall notice in a later analysis, first against the poetised statement as such and second against the poetic experience as such, and it is conducted with intense earnestness. Plato speaks passionately in the tones of a man who feels he is taking on a most formidable opponent who can muster the total forces of tradition and contemporary opinion against him. He pleads, he argues, he denounces, he cajoles. He is a David confronting some Goliath. And he speaks as though he had no choice but to fight the battle to a finish.

There is some mystery here, some historical puzzle. It cannot be solved by pretending it does not exist, that is, by pretending that Plato cannot mean what he says. It is obvious that the poetry he is talking about is not the kind of thing we identify today as poetry. Or more properly that his poetry and our poetry may have a great deal in common, but that what must have changed is the environment in which poetry is practised. Somehow, Plato is talking about an overall cultural condition which no longer exists. What are the clues to this mystery which has so altered our common values that poetry is now esteemed as one of the most inspiring and profitable sources for the cultivation of mind and heart?

Before seeking an answer to this problem it will be necessary to enlarge it. Plato's polemics against poetry are not confined to the first half of the last book. Indeed he reminds us as much in his preface to the book which recalls that poetry 'so far as mimetic' had already been refused acceptance. The reference is to an analysis of the *lexis* or verbal mechanisms of poetry which had been offered in the third book of the *Republic* and which itself followed a previous attack upon poetry's content (*logoi*). This attack had begun before the end of Book Two, when Plato proposed a policy of stern and sweeping censorship of the Greek poets, both past and present. What guidance, he asks himself and his readers, can traditional poetry give us in morality? His answer is: very little; that is, if we take the stories told of the gods, heroes and ordinary men at all seriously. They are full of murder and incest, cruelty and treachery; of passions uncontrolled; of weakness, cowardice and malice. Repetition of such material can only lead to imitation by unformed and tender minds. Censorship is the sole resort. Plato's position is not very different, in short, from those who have advocated a similar editing of the Old Testament for younger readers, except that, the condition of Greek mythology being what it was, his proposals had to be more drastic.

So far, the philosopher's objectives are understandable, whether or not we think they are mistaken. But he then turns from the content of the stories told by the poets to consider the way that they are told. The problem of substance is succeeded by the problem of style, and it is at this point that the sympathetic reader begins to feel mystified. Plato proposes a useful if rather simple classification of poetry under three heads: either it reports what is happening through the mouth of the poet, or it dramatises what is happening by letting the characters speak in their own person, or it does both. Homer is here again in the forefront of the philosopher's mind; he is an exponent of the mixed style, whereas tragedy is wholly devoted to the dramatic. We shall have to notice this analysis more closely in the next chapter. For the present it suffices to observe that Plato obviously is hostile to the dramatic style as such. To be sure, as it turns out, he will tolerate it; that is, he will tolerate the poetry of dramatised situation and speech provided the characters thus presented are ethically superior. But by the time he recalls this context at the beginning of the tenth book he has forgotten he was even as tolerant as that. Through most of what he says in Book Three there persists a strong undercurrent of suspicion and dislike for the dramatic empathy as such. A purely descriptive style he seems to think is always preferable, and he suggests that if Homer were paraphrased to produce a purely descriptive effect, what he is saying would reduce itself to insignificance. We cannot, that is, evade the feeling that even in this discussion, so much less drastic in its proposals than that of Book Ten, Plato is revealing a fundamental hostility to the poetic experience *per se* and to the imaginative act which constitutes such a large part of that experience. And this should be puzzling.

POETRY IN THE *REPUBLIC*

An approach to a solution of the puzzle must begin by first taking the *Republic* as a whole and getting it into perspective, in order to ask: What is the over-all role which poetry plays in this treatise? Is it confined to the passages so far reviewed, which give analytic attention to what the poet says? No, it is not. The formal thesis which is to be demonstrated and defended in the body of the *Republic* is proposed for discussion at the opening of Book Two. 'Socrates' is challenged to isolate the principle of morality in the abstract, and as it may exist as a moral imperative in the soul of man. It is to be defined and defended for its own sake; its rewards or penalties are to be treated as incidental, and it is to be demonstrated that this pure type of morality is the happiest human condition. This challenge dominates the plan of the entire work, and while it is formally answered by the end of Book Nine it continues as the moving cause of the argument of Book Ten.

Why is the challenge so crucial? Surely because it marks an innovation. Such a pure morality has never before been envisaged. What Greece has hitherto enjoyed (says Adeimantus in a passage of great force and sincerity) is a tradition of a half-morality, a sort of twilight zone, at best a compromise, at worst a cynical conspiracy, according to which the younger generation is continually indoctrinated in the view that what is vital is not so much morality as social prestige and material reward which may flow from a moral reputation whether or not this is deserved. Or else (and this is not inconsistent) the young are insensibly warned that virtue is the ideal, of course, but it is difficult and often unrewarding. For the most part a lack of principle proves more profitable. Do not the gods so often reward the unrighteous? And immoral conduct in any case can be expiated quite easily by religious rites. The over-all result is that the Greek adolescent is continually conditioned to an attitude which at bottom is cynical. It is more important to keep up appearances than to practise the reality. Decorum and decent behaviour are not obviously violated, but the inner principle of morality is.

This is an indictment of the Greek tradition and the Greek educational system. The chief authorities cited in support of this type of twilight morality are the poets. Homer and Hesiod are named and quoted, as well as others. It would thus appear that the *Republic* sets itself a problem which is not philosophical in the specialised sense of that term, but rather social and cultural. It questions the Greek tradition as such and the foundations on which it has been built. Crucial to this tradition is the condition and quality of Greek education. That process, whatever it is, by which the mind and attitude of the young are formed lies at the heart of Plato's problem. And at the heart of this process in turn somehow lies the presence of the poets. They are central to the problem. They emerge even here at the beginning of the treatise as 'the enemy', and that is how they are made to play out their role in Book Ten.

Once the *Republic* is viewed as an attack on the existing educational apparatus of Greece, the logic of its total organisation becomes clear. And once it is appreciated that the poets are central to the educational apparatus, the successive critiques of poetry fall into place. That part of the argument which deals directly with political theory occupies only about a third of the nine books, and when it interposes itself, it is to provide successive excuses for progressive discussions of educational theory. The political framework may be utopian; the educational proposals certainly are not. Thus in Book Two, the problem having been proposed, a problem which concerns the construction of justice in the soul of the individual, the device is used of describing first a political society in the large, which shall then correspond to the individual in the small. The evolution of this society is pursued to the point where a 'guardian class' emerges as the key class in the state. Whereupon the argument promptly turns to consider their education, and we get in effect a programme of revised elementary and secondary education for existing Greek practise. This concluded, the argument reverts briefly to politics, in order to describe the three–class state and its virtues in precise detail. Then comes the psychology of the individual soul, a theory obviously devised to conform to Plato's educational objectives. Some more political, social and economic theory then follows—the equality of the sexes, the communisation of the family, and the role of limited war—until the paradox is proposed that the only safe and suitable recipient of political power is the philosopher. This is a novelty. Native philosophers are to say the least a minority group, and their character is defined in explicit contrast to that of the theatregoer, the audience at dramatic performances and the like. Once more, by implication, the poets emerge as the enemy. Then, after a picture of the present ambiguous status of the philosopher in existing societies, according to which he is now a fool and now a criminal, we are confronted with the problem of his proper education, and are introduced to the secret of the fount of true knowledge upon which his intellectual integrity is built. And then in the seventh book, the most important book in the *Republic*, there follows the elaborate curriculum which is to train him for his task. It ascends through mathematics to dialectic, and it is to be made available to the age-group between twenty and thirty-five, and it is to be obtained only on a competitive basis, which at successive stages weeds out the lesser abilities. This concluded, the argument through Book Eight reverts to political theory. The degeneration of societies and of individuals from the ideal is presented in four successive stages before, in Book Nine, Plato returns to his original question. Absolute morality as opposed to current morality has now been defined; it is the condition of the true philosopher. Is it also the happiest condition for men? And after answering yes, Plato in the tenth book turns back to a piece of unfinished business. He had defined the new curriculum of the Academy, but he had not explained the total absence therein of poetry. Its exclusion has now become logical and inevitable for its genius is wholly incompatible with the epistemology which lies behind the new programme. So the poets, revealed briefly in Book Five as the enemies of the philosophers, are now in Book Ten fully exposed and expelled from the discipline that must reign over the philosophic stage of instruction.

From this perspective, the educational argument of the *Republic* moves through two main stages: the primary and secondary curriculum, called *mousike*, and the university curriculum of Book Seven. For each of these, a political excuse is furnished, by the introduction of the guardians in Book Two, and of the philosopher-kings in Book Five. At the first level, the traditional poetic curriculum is to be retained but purged, and purged according to principles which seem to us a little curious; at the second level it is to be unceremoniously thrown out.

This is a great and a splendid argument, a major document in the history of European culture. It marks the introduction of the university system into the west. But it proposes for the modern mind several problems which are historical. Why in the first place, in the existing educational system of Greece, is poetry treated as so absolutely central? It appears, if we are to follow Plato, to enjoy a total monopoly. Why in the second place does Plato propose such curious reforms in the field of poetic style? Why is dramatisation so significant, and why does he think it is so dangerous? And thirdly why does he feel it is essential to throw poetry out of the university curriculum altogether? Which is exactly the place where modern taste and practise find it possible in humane studies to exploit the full possibilities of the poetic experience. Why does Plato feel so committed to a passionate warfare upon the poetic experience as such? The answers to these questions may not be irrelevant to a history of the Greek mind.

MIMESIS

We have spoken of the undercurrent of Plato's hostility to the poetic experience as such—a phenomenon so disconcerting to the Platonist, who may feel that at this point in his thinking the master has let him down. Plato's critique of poetry and the poetic situation is in fact complicated, and it is impossible to understand it unless we are prepared to come to terms with that most baffling of all words in his philosophic vocabulary, the Greek word *mimesis*. In the *Republic* Plato applies it in the first instance as a stylistic classification defining the dramatic as opposed to descriptive composition. But as he goes on he seems to enlarge it to cover several other phenomena. As these are comprehended, some of the clues to the character of the Greek cultural situation begin to emerge.

The word is introduced as he turns in Book Three from the kind of tale narrated by the poet to the problem of the poet's 'technique of verbal communication'. This cumbrous phrase may be adequate to translate the overtones of the Greek word *lexis*, which, as is made clear when Plato proceeds, covers the entire verbal apparatus, rhythmic and imagistic, at the poet's disposal. The critique which now follows, on careful inspection, divides into three parts. Plato begins by examining the case of the poet *per se*, his style of composition and the effects he may achieve. In the middle of his argument he switches to consider problems connected with the psychology of the 'guardians', that is, of his citizen soldiers, problems which he regards as related, but which certainly pertain to a different class in the community, for citizen soldiers cannot be said by any stretch of the imagination to be poets. Later still, he turns back again to the problem of poetic composition and style, and the poet rather than the guardian once more occupies the field of vision. Let us survey first what is said in the two passages on the poets and their poetry.

Plato begins by arguing in effect that in all verbal communication there is a fundamental distinction between the descriptive method and that of dramatisation. Homer is still the prototype of both. His poems divide into the speeches which are exchanged, as between actors, and the statements which intervene, spoken by the poet in person. The former are examples of *mimesis*, of dramatic 'imitation' or 'impersonation', the latter are examples of 'simple rehearsal' or as we might say, straight narrative in the third person. Epic is thus *in toto* an example of the mixed mode of composition, whereas drama exemplifies only mimetic composition. Plato's words make it clear that he is not interested in the distinction between epic and tragedy as genres, which we find familiar, but in basic types of verbal communication. Drama according to his classification is comprehended under epic, as is narrative. He hints as much when, in answer to the suggestion of Adeimantus that he is preparing to exclude drama from his ideal state, he replies: 'Perhaps; but perhaps also my target is bigger. I don't yet know. We have to proceed whither the logic of our argument carries us': a hint which looks forward to the more fundamental critique of Book Ten, and warns us that the formal distinction between epic and drama is not in itself relevant to his philosophic purpose.

So far, we conclude, the term *mimesis* has been usefully and rather precisely applied to define a method of composition. But there is slipped in, during the course of this part of the argument, a very curious statement: 'When the poet speaks a speech in the person of another, he makes his verbal medium (*lexis*) resemble the speaker'—and then Plato continues: 'Any poet who makes himself resemble another in voice or gesture is imitating him' (and hence practising *mimesis*). Now, this on the face of it is a *non-sequitur*. The missing link which has slipped out between these two statements would run as follows: 'Any poet who makes his verbal medium resemble the speaker is making himself resemble the speaker.' Now this, if applied to the creative act of composition on the part of the poet, is patently untrue. The poet applies his conscious skill to choosing words temporarily appropriate to Agamemnon. So far from 'imitating Agamemnon in his own character, he must keep his own artistic integrity detached, for in a moment the same skill is to be employed to put appropriate words in the mouth of Achilles. But Plato's supposition would be approximately true if it were applied not to the creation of a poem but to an actor or reciter who recites it. He in a measure does have to 'identify' with the original supplied to him by the creative artist. He has to throw himself into the part precisely because he is not creating it but reproducing it, and this reproduction is for the benefit of an audience whose interest and attention he must engage. He can refuse to 'imitate', and get only a lukewarm response.

The first puzzle concerning *mimesis* as the word is used by Plato has now already appeared. Why use it to describe both an act of composition which constitutes an act of creation, and a performance by an actor who is a mouthpiece or a reciter? Is this a loose and confusing use of the word, or is Plato expressing faithfulness to a cultural situation which is alien to our own?

When in the last third of his argument Plato returns to the poet's case, the ambiguity between the situation of the creative artist and that of the actor or performer is maintained. It is impossible to be sure which of them in any given sentence is more prominently before the philosopher's eye. Considered as an 'orator', our Platonic poet will prefer a style with a minimum of *mimesis* and a maximum of description. His indulgence in extreme forms of *mimesis*, extending even to the growls and squeals of animals, will be in direct proportion to his inferiority as a poet. And then Plato adds a comment which is in part a stylistic analysis and in part a philosophic judgment: 'The dramatic-mimetic mode involves all-various shapes of changes.' It is polymorphous and, we might say, exhibits the characteristics of a rich and unpredictable flux of experience. The descriptive mode cuts this tendency down to a minimum. Are we then to admit the performance of that kind of versatile poet whose skill can enable him to be any kind of person and to represent any and everything? Emphatically no. Clearly, then, the situation of the creative artist and of the performer of a work of art still overlap each other in Plato's mind.

But this peroration raises still another problem which we have touched on in the previous chapter. Why is the philosopher so profoundly hostile to the range and versatility which dramatisation makes possible? It has been argued that his target is merely the extreme and uncouth realism of some contemporaries. But philosophic objection is taken to variety and range in principle, and will apply to good drama as well as bad. How comes it that a poetic virtue (in our eyes) which enlarges both range of meaning in the product and emotional sympathy in the audience is converted by Plato precisely into a vice?

In the intervening section of his argument Plato suddenly turns from the poets and performers to consider the young guardians of his state, and applies the mimetic situation to their case. Are they to be mimetic? he asks. Now they presumably are not going to be either poets or actors, but citizen soldiers, and in that case, how can the problem of *mimesis*, if it be a matter of artistic style and method, affect them at all? The clue lies in the 'occupations', 'pursuits', 'procedures', or 'practices' (all of these are possible translations of the single Greek word *epitedeumata*) which are admittedly central to the life of these young men. They have as adults to become 'craftsmen of freedom' for the state. But they also have to learn this trade, and they learn by practise and by performance, in fact by an education in which they are trained to 'imitate' previous models of behaviour. Hence *mimesis* now becomes a term applied to the situation of a student apprentice, who absorbs lessons, and repeats and hence 'imitates' what he is told to master. The point is made all the clearer when Plato recalls that earlier social and educational principle which required division of labour and specialisation. The young guardians pose a problem of training. Their assigned task will not be narrowly technical but one which requires character and ethical judgment. These he says are precisely the result of a training which employs constant 'imitation' carried out 'from boyhood'. Clearly therefore the context of the argument has shifted from the artistic situation to the educational one. But this only complicates still further the mystery of the ambivalence of *mimesis*. Why should Plato, not content with applying the same word both to the creation and to the performance of the poem, also apply it to the learning act achieved by a pupil? Why in fact are the situations of artist, of actor and of pupil confused? Nor does this exhaust the ambiguities of the word. For as he warms to his theme of the pupil-guardian and how his moral condition depends on the correct kind of 'imitations', the pupil seems to turn into a grown man who for some reason is continually engaged in reciting or performing poetry himself which may involve him in unfortunate types of imitation. He had better, says Plato, be on his guard to censor his own performance. In short, not only is the poetic situation confused with the educational, but the educational is then confused with the recreational, if that is the correct word by which to describe the mood of adult recitation.

It is therefore not much wonder if scholars and critics have had difficulty in deciding precisely what Plato does mean by *mimesis*. And before we leave Book Three, there is still one more complication we have to notice. The word as introduced was used to define only one *eidos* or species of composition, namely the dramatic, to which was opposed both the 'simple' style of direct narration and the 'mixed' style which employs the two together. To this meaning it adheres through most of the argument on style. But before the end is reached, Adeimantus without objection from Socrates can speak of that 'imitation of a virtuous model which is simple'. Is this a slip, or are we to infer that imitation is a term which is also applicable to non-dramatic types of poetry? And so to all poetry *qua* poetry?

This is precisely the turn given to the word as the argument of Book Ten unfolds itself. True, the poetry to be banned is at first qualified as 'poetry in so far as it is mimetic,' but this qualification then appears to be dropped. Plato as he says himself has now sharpened his vision of what poetry really is. He has transcended the critique of Book Three, which confined itself to drama as its target. Now, not only the dramatist, but Homer and Hesiod come into question. Nor is the issue any longer confined to protecting the moral character. The danger is one of crippling the intellect. And why this? The answer, he replies, will require a complete and exhaustive definition of what *mimesis* really amounts to. This answer depends on whether we accept the Platonic doctrine, established in the intervening books, that absolute knowledge, or true science if we so choose to call it, is of the Forms and of the Forms alone, and that applied science or skilled technique depends on copying the Forms in artifacts. The painter and the poet achieve neither. Poetry is not so much non-functional as anti-functional. It totally lacks the precise knowledge that a craftsman for example can apply to his trade, still less can it employ the precise aims and goals which guide the skilled educator in his training of the intellect. For this training depends on the skill of calculation and measurement; the illusions of sensible experience are critically corrected by the controlling reason. Poetry *per contra* indulges in constant illusionism, confusion and irrationality. This is what *mimesis* ultimately is, a shadow-show of phantoms, like those images seen in the darkness on the wall of the cave.

We have summarised the decisive part of this argument. In a later chapter we shall return to it in more detail. But it is now obvious that *mimesis* has become the word *par excellence* for the over-all linguistic medium of the poet and his peculiar power through the use of this medium (meter and imagery are included in the attack) to render an account of reality. For Plato, reality is rational, scientific and logical, or it is nothing. The poetic medium, so far from disclosing the true relations of things or the true definitions of the moral virtues, forms a kind of refracting screen which disguises and distorts reality and at the same time distracts us and plays tricks with us by appealing to the shallowest of our sensibilities.

So *mimesis* is now the total act of poetic representation, and no longer simply the dramatic style. On what grounds could Plato apply the same word first in the narrower sense and then in the broader? And how, we repeat, can we explain in this broader sense the fundamental philosophic hostility to the poetic experience as such?

As he dissects the poetic account, so he also seeks to define that part of our consciousness to which it is designed to appeal, and to which the poetic language and rhythm are addressed. This is the area of the non-rational, of the pathological emotions, the unbridled and fluctuating sentiments with which we feel but never think. When indulged in this way they can weaken and destroy that rational faculty in which alone lies hope of personal salvation and also scientific assurance. *Mimesis* has just been applied to the content of the poetised statement. But as he considers the appeal of this kind of statement to our consciousness, he is drawn back into portraying the pathology of the audience at a performance of poetry, and *mimesis* resumes one of those meanings it had assumed in Book Three. It now is the name of the active personal identification by which the audience sympathises with the performance. It is the name of our submission to the spell. It describes no longer the artist's imperfect vision, whatever that may be, but the identification of the audience with that vision.

For this meaning of *mimesis*, Book Three, we repeat, had prepared us, and if Plato had used the word only or mainly in this sense we would have less difficulty in understanding the usage. 'Imitation', regarded as a form of impersonation, is an understandable conception. Though we might argue that the good actor may recreate his part anew, in general his performance is readily viewed as an act of imitation. We raise our eyebrows, or should, at the further application of the word to the involvement of the audience in a performance. Plato's descriptions in this context have a ring of mob psychology about them. They do not sound too much like the mood and attitude in which modern theatregoers attend a play, still less like the kind of attention a pupil gives to his lesson. We in fact have to notice here a hint of a curious emotionalism on the part of the Greeks which is alien to our experience. It is all part of the larger puzzle still unresolved.

But nothing is quite so hard to digest, if modern values and sensibilities are taken into account, as that picture of *mimesis* which Plato gives when he applies the word to the very content of the poetic communication, the genius of the poetised experience. Why on earth, we wish to ask, should he attempt to judge poetry as though it were science or philosophy or mathematics or technology? Why demand that the poet 'know', in the sense that the carpenter knows about a bed? Surely this is to degrade the standards of poetic creation by submitting them to criteria which are unworthy or at least improper and irrelevant. Need the poet be an expert in the matter that he sings of? Such a presupposition does not make sense.

This however is precisely the supposition that Plato in Book Ten adopts without question and it brings us to confront our last and most crucial problem in the search for clues as to what all this means. We saw in our review of the treatise as a whole that, as educational theory is central to the plan of the *Republic*, so also poetry is central in the educational theory. It occupied this position so it seems in contemporary society, and it was a position held apparently not on the grounds that we would offer, namely poetry's inspirational and imaginative effects, but on the ground that it provided a massive repository of useful knowledge, a sort of encyclopedia of ethics, politics, history and technology which the effective citizen was required to learn as the core of his educational equipment. Poetry represented not something we call by that name, but an indoctrination which today would be comprised in a shelf of text books and works of reference.

Plato in the tenth book is quite explicit: 'Our next task is a critical examination of tragedy and Homer the prototype thereof. We are told in certain quarters that these poets possess the know-how of all techniques and all human affairs pertaining to vice and virtue, not to mention divine matters.' These claims in Plato's eyes are impossible to maintain. Let us however, he says, ignore for the moment the claim to technical competence and come instead 'to those major matters of supreme value on which Homer undertakes to speak, warfare, military leadership, politics and administration, and the education of men'. Thus phrased, the claim becomes Homer's own. That is, Plato is reporting the traditional estimate placed upon his poetry, and that estimate crystallised itself in the conception of Homer as the Hellenic educational manual *par excellence*. He proceeds to expose it as false and asks rhetorically 'if he had really been able to educate men and make them better, . . . then who have been his pupils and his protégés?' The Sophists have their following, which at least proves their educational effectiveness. But where are Homer's followers, or Hesiod's?

The question sounds too much like an *argumentum ad hominem*. Plato at any rate turns from rhetoric back to dialectic, and proceeds to demonstrate at length the complete gulf between the truth, as understood by reason, and the illusions effected by poetry. And then, as he begins to approach the terminus of his polemic, he cites once more that conception of Homer which he finds so impossible: 'When you encounter encomiasts of Homer who say that this poet has educated Hellas for the purpose of administration of human affairs and of education therein; that he is the correct authority to be taken up and learnt, since this poet can guide the conduct of man's entire life . . .'— in the face of this claim one can only reply gently—'You may be as good a man as is possible under the circumstances . . .' (that is, as a product of Homeric education); but nevertheless, Homer as we have him is not admissible. Yet how hard it is to do this, exclaims Plato. Don't we all feel Homer's spell? But still our feeling for him, though traditional and deep, is a love that we have to renounce, so dangerous it is:

'Our *eros* for this kind of poetry is bred in us by the educational nurture characteristic of the better polities.' But it is perilous, and we shall say over to ourselves our rational antidote to it, 'taking great care less we fall back again into this immature passion which the many still feel'.

It is clear from these statements that the poets in general and Homer in particular were not only considered as the source of instruction in ethics and administrative skills but also enjoyed a sort of institutional status in Greek society. This status received, as it were, state support, because they supplied a training which the social and political mechanism relied on for its efficient working.

All this forces us to realise that Plato assumes among his contemporaries a view of the poet and his poetry which is wholly unfamiliar to our way of thinking. We assume that the poet is an artist and his products are works of art. Plato seems at one point to think so too, when he compares the poet to the visual artist, the painter. But he does not make this comparison on aesthetic grounds. In fact, it is not too much to say that the notion of the aesthetic as a system of values which might apply to literature and to artistic composition never once enters the argument. Plato writes as though he had never heard of aesthetics, or even of art. Instead he insists on discussing the poets as though their job was to supply metrical encyclopedias. The poet is a source on the one hand of essential information and on the other of essential moral training. Historically speaking, his claims even extend to giving technical instruction. It is as though Plato expected poetry to perform all those functions which we relegate on the one hand to religious instruction or moral training and on the other to classroom texts, to histories and handbooks, to encyclopedias and reference manuals. This is a way of looking at poetry which in effect refuses to discuss it as poetry in our sense at all. It refuses to allow that it may be an art with its own rules rather than a source of information and a system of indoctrination.

This is to us an astonishing assumption, but once accepted, it provides the logical excuse for Plato to apply to poetry that philosophic critique which he does by placing poetry in relation to the Theory of Forms. The Theory is epistemological; it seeks to define the character of that knowledge which we would call universal, exact and final. Mathematical science will in this instance suffice as an example. Applied science is not alien to this theoretic kind of knowledge. On the contrary it applies it by using the unique and exact Forms as models which are copied in existing material products. Beds in the plural are the carpenter's copies of the unique Form of bed. But the poet simply talks about a bed in his poetry without knowing anything about it or attempting to make it. This kind of argument is perhaps fair to Homer if Homer is really pretending to be a manual on the manufacture of beds and the like. For if so it is a bad manual, says Plato. It is not composed by that kind of man who technically understands beds or ships or horses or anything else. On the contrary what he is doing is simply painting word-portraits of what beds look like in a thousand different confusing situations and he is effective only in the illusions he is able to create by verbal and rhythmic images, not in exact procedures for manufacture.

This is the 'mimesis at second remove' to which Plato consigns the poet in the more fundamental part of his critique in Book Ten. This use of *mimesis* essentially indicates that the poetic statement is mummery; it is illusionism, as opposed to the carpenter's mechanical exactitude and faithfulness, and the term is applied to the entire basic content of the poetised statement as such and not just to drama.

Such is the last and final metamorphosis of *mimesis* at Plato's hands. It is truly a protean word. But behind the puzzle of its application in the sense of total poetic illusionism is that second puzzle which gives rise to the first. This is, we repeat, to us the astonishing presumption that poetry was conceived and intended to be a kind of social encyclopedia. If it was so designed, it was obviously by Plato's day doing a very poor job. It could not carry out this task according to the standards which Plato required in the Academy. The hallmark of his own curriculum is conveyed in the Greek term *episteme* for which our word science is one possible equivalent. The graduate of the Platonic academy has passed through a rigorous training in mathematics and logic which has equipped him to define the aims of human life in scientific terms and to carry them out in a society which has been reorganised upon scientific lines. The poet as a possible claimant to fulfil this role thus becomes an easy target; we feel too easy. He should never have been placed in such an inappropriate position in the first place. Plato should never have done this to him. But he does do it, and we have to ask why.

THE MYTH
OF ER*

I.M. Crombie

Socrates closes the discussion by relating a myth or fable, as he does also in the *Gorgias* and *Phaedo*. Myths and fables are fairly common in the dialogues, some long and elaborate, some quite short. They have a number of different functions; some (for example the story about the invention of writing, *Phaedrus* 274–5) are simply fables like Aesop's designed to express pictorially in a story what could equally well have been said without it. Others however, particularly those concerned with eschatology, are rather different. Of these we might say that the purpose of the story is that the reader may, by the process of 'drawing the moral', learn the region within which in Plato's view the truth is to be found. Where he is unable or unwilling to state a precise doctrine an author may, by telling a story, bring alive what would otherwise be vague generalisations. In this sense the whole of the *Timaeus*, in my view, may be regarded as a myth, since its purpose is to show that it is credible that the world is rationally ordered, and its method is to give an account of its constitution, the details of which are not (I think) to be taken seriously, the purpose of giving the account being to give the reader some idea of the *kind* of account the truth of which would justify the claim that the world is rationally ordered, to put some content into the notion of rational order. To some extent similar remarks apply to the *Republic* as a whole. For in the political sections of this dialogue, as I have several times suggested, Plato's purpose is not to tell us what a wonderful community a philosopher could create if he had a community of children under ten to mould how he wished, but, by describing such a community, to urge the validity of certain principles, in particular that politics is a

* From *An Examination of Plato's Doctrines*, Vol. I, by I.M. Crombie (New York, 1962), pp. 153–155. Reprinted by permission of The Humanities Press.

vain business unless it is subordinated to an understanding of the good for man. A myth then, of the kind to which the eschatological myths of the *Gorgias*, *Phaedo*, and *Republic* belong, is a story such that, if that story were true, that would be an implementation of certain principles. Thus for example, if, after death, we had to choose our next life in the manner described by Er the Armenian in the present myth, that would be an implementation of the principle that a man is responsible, through what he lets himself become in one incarnation, for the form that his next earthly life will take. Unfortunately however it would also be an implementation of the vaguer principle that we are responsible, through the effect which our choices have upon our characters, for what happens to us in life. This indicates a general difficulty, from the reader's point of view, in the mythical inculcation of truths; one knows that some details are to be discounted, but one does not know how many. If, in the present example, one thinks that reincarnation is to be discounted, then one will say that it is the vaguer principle which is being conveyed; if on the other hand reincarnation is not part of the story, but part of the moral, then it will be the more precise principle that we are supposed to derive. However this may be (and I am confident that the second alternative is in fact correct in this case) we may say that the general purpose of a myth of this kind is to convey a principle by describing *one* way in which that principle might be implemented. At the same time however some of the major myths are certainly designed to be impressive, to drive a moral lesson home through an appeal to the imagination. In such myths Plato's style changes; his sentences become more elaborate and highly fashioned, he becomes elliptical and allusive—his frustrated poetic gifts are allowed their freedom. Finally since a myth is what it is, the author of an eschatological myth has an opportunity, in constructing his *mise-en-scène*, to put forward cosmological and astronomical ideas without committing himself to their truth, an opportunity which in this case Plato takes.

To me these myths tremble between the sublime and the tedious; but I shall not spoil the *Republic* myth for those who might appreciate it by giving a summary. Its bones however are these. After this life we are rewarded or punished for the things that we have done on earth, incurable sinners being thrown for ever into Tartarus. Retribution over, the rest of us are made to choose our next life from a pool of lives. Of these there are enough for everybody to find a tolerable life, if only he knows how to choose. It is our fault, and not God's, if we choose badly. This choice takes place at the 'spindle of Necessity', an imaginary axis around which the heavens rotate; and the choice, once made, is binding, as befits a choice made at such a place. The lives between which we have to choose ('biographies' might be a better word for them) are incomplete in one respect; we do not choose our moral characters. We choose our status, human or animal, we choose beauty or ugliness, wealth or poverty, the incidents of our lives. We do not choose character because that is entailed by the choice of externals that we make. It is here, Socrates breaks off to tell Glaucon, that the whole of human life is in the balance. It is because character is determined by the choice of externals that it is above all other knowledge essential to know what causes produce what moral effects in human life—how beauty or strength or high birth or political power affect a man, what are the results produced by the various combinations of such factors as these on the different kinds of moral character. These things must be assessed 'looking to the nature of the soul and deeming evil that which makes a man unjust, good that which makes him just'. It is essential that we give our minds to this study while we can, for the choices made by the discarnate souls are often misguided. Those for example who have been in their previous incarnation conventionally virtuous, and whose discarnate condition has therefore been easy, may well make disastrous choices just because they have no experience of tribulation. Only philosophy, because it involves an understanding of human life, can protect us against the risk of such errors.

The concluding paragraph exhorts us, through justice and wisdom, to seek prosperity in this life and thereafter. It is, like others of Plato's concluding paragraphs, a supreme piece of prose by which the reader finds himself swept away, even while he admires its dignity and restraint. The last words, bearing the weight of the whole dialogue, are: 'That we may prosper.'

The crux of the myth is of course Socrates' aside to Glaucon, in which Plato condenses the ethical teaching of the whole dialogue, and indeed provides an explanation of it which he has been keeping up his sleeve almost until now. We now know what it is the knowledge of which enables just men to contribute what is fitting—the question with which Socrates perplexed Polemarchus at the beginning of the dialogue. It is by knowing, implicitly or explicitly, how various combinations of moral character and external circumstance affect the further building up of character that just men are able to make wise choices for themselves or for others. It is because such knowledge must be explicit if it is to be capable of application in all circumstances that there can be no cessation of evils until power is in the hands of the philosophers.

The dialogue ends on the theme with which it began, the validity of moral rules. It is because what he does affects a man's character and thereby his true welfare that it makes sense to commend certain kinds of conduct and to condemn others. Whatever truth there may be in Thrasymachus' or Glaucon's account of the origin of morality, this is its justification.

Suggested Further Readings

Millions of words have been written about the *Republic*, from Plato's time to the present. We list here only a few general works and a small number of the books and articles concerned specifically with the *Republic*. An extensive bibliography of recent writings on Plato may be found in the *Classical Weekly*, Vol. 50 (1957).

COMPLETE COLLECTIONS OF PLATO'S DIALOGUES

The Dialogues of Plato, edited by E. Hamilton and H. Cairns (New York, 1961).

The Dialogues of Plato, translated by B. Jowett (4th edition), 4 volumes (Oxford, 1953).

INEXPENSIVE EDITIONS OF THE *REPUBLIC*

The Republic of Plato, translated with introduction and notes by F. M. Cornford (New York, 1945). The most widely used edition of the *Republic*.

The Republic and Other Works, translated by B. Jowett (New York, 1960).

The Portable Plato, translated by B. Jowett (New York, 1948).

Plato: Republic, translated by H. D. P. Lee (Baltimore, 1955).

GENERAL WORKS ON PLATO'S PHILOSOPHY

R. S. Brumbaugh, *Plato for the Modern Age* (New York, 1962).

I. M. Crombie, *An Examination of Plato's Doctrines* (New York, 1962).

R. Crossman, *Plato Today* (Oxford, 1959).

G. C. Field, *Plato and His Contemporaries* (London, 1930).

Paul Friedlander, *Plato* (New York, 1958).

M. A. Grube, *Plato's Thought* (London, 1935).

R. Levinson, *In Defense of Plato* (Cambridge, 1953).

K. Popper, *The Open Society* (Princeton, 1945).

Richard Robinson, *Plato's Earlier Dialectic* (Oxford, 1953).

Sir David Ross, *Plato's Theory of Ideas* (Oxford, 1953).

Leo Strauss, *The City and Man* (Chicago, 1964).

A. E. Taylor, *Plato, the Man and His Work* (New York, 1926).
T. L. Thorson, *Plato: Totalitarian or Democrat* (Englewood Cliffs, 1963).
E. Voegelin, *Order and History*, volume III (Baton Rouge, 1957).
F. J. E. Woodbridge, *The Son of Apollo* (Boston, 1929).

WRITINGS CONCERNED PRIMARILY WITH THE *REPUBLIC*

Ernest Barker, *The Political Thought of Plato and Aristotle* (New York, 1906).
B. Bosanquet, *A Companion to Plato's Republic* (New York, 1895).
R. C. Cross and A. D. Woozley, *Plato's Republic: A Philosophical Commentary* (New York, 1964).
E. Havelock, *Preface to Plato* (Cambridge, 1963).
Werner Jaeger, *Paideia*, volume II (New York, 1943).
H. W. B. Joseph, *Ancient and Modern Philosophy* (Oxford, 1935).
N. R. Murphy, *The Interpretation of Plato's Republic* (Oxford, 1951).
R. L. Nettleship, *Lectures on the Republic of Plato* (New York, 1901).
R. S. Bluck, "Plato's Ideal State," *Classical Quarterly*, 9 (1959).
R. Demos, "Paradoxes in Plato's Doctrine of the Ideal State," *Classical Quarterly*, 7 (1957).
W. C. Greene, "The Paradoxes of the *Republic*," *Harvard Studies in Classical Philology*, 63 (1958).
R. W. Hall, "Justice and the Individual in the *Republic*," *Phronesis*, 4 (1959).
R. G. Hoerber, "Note on the Structure of the *Republic*," *Phronesis*, 6 (1961).
G. F. Hourani, "Thrasymachus' Definition of Justice in the *Republic*," *Phronesis*, 7 (1962).
I. C. Lieb, "Philosophy as Spiritual Formation: Plato's Myth of Er," *International Philosophical Quarterly*, 3 (1964).
S. Rosen, "The Role of Eros in Plato's *Republic*," *Review of Metaphysics*, xviii (1965).
R. Weingartner, "Vulgar Justice and Platonic Justice," *Philosophy and Phenomenological Research*, xxv (1964–5).

A. W. H. Adkins' *Merit and Responsibility* (Oxford, 1960) contains a valuable discussion of some aspects of the *Republic*, but this is not readily intelligible apart from a reading of the whole book, which is an excellent account of the development of Greek moral thought.